Centerville Library
Washington-Centerville Public Librar
Centerville Ohio
DISCARD

D1544002

Boxing fitness

A system of training for complete boxing fitness

Ian Oliver

Strength and conditioning professional, Bob Breen's Academy of Martial Arts,
Hoxton Square, London.
www.bobbreen.co.uk

With photographs by Pete Drinkell and Anna Torborg

Copyright © 2004 Ian Oliver

Advanced training section © 2005 Ian Oliver

The Author asserts the moral right to be identified
as the author of this work.

All rights reserved.

2006

4

Proudly published by

Snowbooks Ltd.

120 Pentonville Road

London

N1 9JN

Tel: 0207 837 6482

Fax: 0207 837 6348

email: info@snowbooks.com

www.snowbooks.com

British Library Cataloguing in Publication Data

A catalogue record for this book is available from the British Library.

ISBN 9780954575984

Contents

Acknowledgements

Kind thanks to my colleague Victoria Mose from the YMCA training and development department for ensuring the accuracy of the advice that follows.

Also to my good friend Savash Mustafa (Doctor of Osteopathy) for his kind assurance that the training regimes contained within are not life threatening.

Grateful acknowledgements must also go to Emma Cahill, Pete Drinkell and my good friend and colleague Wayne Rowlands who made this book a reality instead of a possibility; and to Sally and Cheryl, whose constant moaning forced my hand.

Respect and special thanks go out to Bob Breen, Terry Barnett, Gordon McAdam and Alex Turnbull, from all of whose motivational classes I borrowed so heavily, and still continue to do so.

A word of warning

It almost goes without saying that a book on boxing training will involve some vigorous and demanding physical effort. If you have any concerns about your health then I must stress the importance of getting clearance from your doctor. If you have not participated in any training before, or not for some time, then start gradually, always taking the easier options and limiting the training times. Too many people have the impression that if exercise doesn't hurt then it is not achieving anything: this is not the case. You should, and my fervent hope is that you will, enjoy your exercise. Never forget that you have the rest of your life to get fit.

Note from Terry Barnett

A practical book on boxing fitness is long overdue in the martial arts world and Ian Oliver is eminently qualified to produce such a guide. Ian's approach to the 'noble art' is the same as his approach to life: a down-to-earth, no-nonsense view supported by superior levels of intelligence and humility.

Those of us who have been lucky enough to train under Ian have marvelled at his wealth of knowledge and his ability to express and share his experiences. He has the ability to make the complex seem simple and is constantly adding to his seemingly endless repertoire of drills.

Those reading this book who know Ian will not be surprised at the quality of what is to follow. Those who have never met him should prepare themselves for a wonderful journey of discovery.

Terry Barnett

Note from Rick Faye

It's about time that someone put together a boxing book like this for martial artists. Ian's expertise in caring for his students comes out in every page, and even the smallest tips are essential in the gym. This is a must have for every martial arts book collection.

Rick Faye

Foreword from Bob Breen

Boxing is an amazing art and science. Here theory and practice fight it out on a nightly basis. Part poetry of movement, part brutality, the lure of boxing to modern man is very strong. Here one can test oneself in ritual conflict, and for many even light sparring can be a rite of passage. The training is wholesome and complete, building lean bodies and, most often, minds devoid of aggression and fear. I find it incredible that some sort of boxing, perhaps of a less destructive nature, isn't part of the sports curriculum in all schools.

However, to progress well in this art you need a good trainer and I know few better and more passionate than Ian Oliver. Ian is a unique individual; not only a good and very knowledgeable coach with a huge interest in boxing, but erudite and widely read on almost any subject. He brings fun and enthusiasm and a down-to-earth ease to all his classes and I'm glad that this ease and fun has been carried over to this book. It's not as good as training with the man himself, but nearly. Thoroughly recommended.

Bob Breen

Dedication

This book is dedicated to all instructors, staff and students
of the Bob Breen Academy past and present, all my family
(especially my long-suffering wife Brenda) and to the memory
of John McDavid, Laura Logan, "Wink" Walker, Roy Beckworth,
Johnny Bird and F. S. O.

*But to those who have their bodies in good condition, there is
great assurance from danger, and no danger of suffering any such
calamity from weakness of constitution.*

(from *The Memorabilia of Socrates*)

I. Introduction

The majority of people who read this are not interested in boxing as a profession, or even as a highly competitive amateur; those people started out as kids, or at least teenagers. They have honed their skills the hard way, taught by seasoned trainers who know how to get them battle-hardened, while keeping them within the confines of a particular weight.

Ian Oliver

This book is for those who want to get fit using boxing training as a conduit, as opposed to simply using weight training, aerobics, running or other activities that they feel have lost their stimulus as stand-alone exercises. Participants have never failed to surprise me. In the past I have trained actors, dancers, doormen, executives, artists, musicians, DJs, lawyers and professional sportspeople.

In my experience, there are a few fundamental reasons why people turn to boxing.

They want something new in the way of training that will be demanding but refreshing. No matter how placid people are by nature, most of them still feel great enjoyment from hitting something hard. A middle-aged, physically disabled lady would come into the gym for 20 minutes on quiet afternoons to simply punch the heavy bag in 16 oz. gloves. She would leave in a calm, serene mood, telling us how much better she felt. Taking out your frustration and anger on a punchbag is a great form of psychological self-help. Buy a punchbag and sack your analyst; what better form of anger management can there be? Cheaper too, even with gym membership.

They feel they would like a shot at "white collar" boxing competition, in what was once more of a blue collar sport. Schools do not teach boxing: it became considered decadent and politically incorrect years ago. Only the forces and some universities still encourage it. Oxford and Cambridge have an annual Varsity match, and there is a boxing union student federation. One of our students, Rob Howard, a former Oxford Boxing Blue who goes back to Oxford to help with training, has since moved into white collar competition and is, as yet, unbeaten. Boxing clubs, even for youngsters, are few and far between; they do not usually generate much revenue, and rising rents and other outgoings have sadly forced many clubs to close. Years ago these clubs did not have to compete with home computers and karate clubs for their membership.

They are not looking to get a huge build, but seek the lithe, muscular look that fighters develop, as opposed to body-builders. Despite the claim of many other martial arts, boxing is still seen as the prime means of self-defence. You get two-for-one on this score as you become able to fight, and in condition to do so as well.

As part of, or as an introduction to, a martial art or integrated martial art, such as muay thai, Panantukan, kickboxing, Vale Tudo and Jeet Kune Do.

Boxing has become regarded in the media as a minority sport, covering only major contests, usually involving heavyweights. Its resurgence has come from public interest in doing it instead of watching it. A few years ago, the high-tech gyms would never have included a punchbag among their glittering array of shiny machines, but clients wanted them, and they wanted to know how to skip rope like a fighter. New gyms are springing up which include rows of bags and even boxing rings. Contemporary films about boxing include *The Cinderella Man* (Russell Crowe), *Against the Ropes* (Meg Ryan), *The Calcium Kid* (Orlando Bloom) and *Million Dollar Baby* (Clint Eastwood and Hilary Swank), but don't just watch it, give it a try.

Boxing and the Bob Breen Academy

It was Jeet Kune Do (JKD) which re-awakened my interest in boxing; the way we teach at the Academy is generally referred to as Western Boxing, which differentiates it from the many other forms of boxing. It is taught as the first and most basic element of the many-faceted art of JKD, devised by Bruce Lee, continued principally by Dan Inosanto, his friend and student, and popularised in the UK by Bob Breen, himself a student of Sifu Inosanto. Bruce Lee believed in training incredibly hard, pushing himself to the limit. He ran, he skipped, he weight-trained, he worked out on punchbags and pads and he cycled, mostly flat out!

At the Academy we use all the same training skills, plus a few more, as more modern thinking and innovations are absorbed. Overtraining is something to always be aware of; some people actually have to be told to cut back their training before their over-enthusiasm makes them ill. It is one thing to venerate Bruce Lee; it would be inadvisable to copy his full training regime.

I have been teaching and training at the Academy for nearly 20 years (sad soul that I am), and have enjoyed its terrific atmosphere and ambience, as well as its complete absence of elitism, sexism, racism and, luckily for me, ageism.

Boxing for all

My speciality has always been specific conditioning, whether it was for martial arts, boxing, soccer, rugby, skiing, tennis or just personal training to get in good shape. I have no preconceptions about which people are best suited to which sport. If you fancy having a go at boxing, why wait until you are older, fitter or lighter? It is a sport—or art, whichever way you look at it—in which you will get fitter by participation at even the lowest level. It is not until you have dipped your toes in the water that you will determine how deep you want to go in, and how far from the shore you want to strike out.

I have been pleasantly surprised by the increasing number of women who now enjoy not just boxing training, but sparring as well, usually with the guys. These girls are fit and strong, and capable of defending themselves, as is sadly required in some of our urban areas. If any of my female students read this and think I am being patronising, I can only say one thing: please don't hit me!

Technique

I will touch only briefly on technique in Chapter 2, as that would need a book in itself. I have therefore simply outlined the basic punches to help with working on pads and bags.

I sincerely believe you can learn to train from a book, but you cannot learn to fight from one: you need to get to a gym. Even the best book on golf cannot teach you how to hit a decent drive; a cricket book cannot prepare you to face a fast bowler and a book on cycling cannot show you how to ride a bike. The best boxing technique book I have come across is still *The Lonsdale Boxing Manual* by the late David James: although 10 years or so old, it will advise you on punching and defending, but the theory is only a small percentage of what you need. The actual practical application is paramount.

Why boxing?

Boxing will improve strength (of both body and character), speed, aerobic and anaerobic fitness, agility, and muscular and cardiovascular endurance, as well as providing a means of self-defence.

What sort of boxing?

This is not the boxing of Las Vegas or the Royal Albert Hall, but boxing as a form of martial art, hopefully with the spirit, values and mutual respect that can usually be found in genuine martial arts training.

Why a book on boxing training?

Every day at the gym with my fellow instructors, Wayne, Dave and Owen, we are fielding questions on the best way to train. The more dedicated students write information down, or get one of us to. It was the girls in the office who first moaned at me to write a book, and my original intention was to set it all down for the students at the Academy. For all I know they may be the only readership I ever get! If this helps anybody get fitter and healthier, I will feel the effort has been worthwhile. If it gets somebody into a gym, working out on the heavy bag, I will be extremely pleased.

Happy training.

2. Technique

The information given is for right-handers, setting up with the left foot forward. If you are left-handed, my apologies; just reverse all right and left-handed instructions.

Do not forget what the basic aim must be: hit but avoid being hit back. Never, even when working on bags or pads, hang around to admire your handiwork. Remember this crude but useful maxim favoured by the old school: hit and hop it!

The stance

2.1 The stance

Imagine you are standing on a large clockface, your left foot on 12 o' clock and your right foot at twenty past twelve. You will try to maintain this stance for most of the time you are boxing, making sure you never cross your feet.

Your bodyweight leans minimally forward from the waist. You are not bolt upright but slightly crouched. Your chin is low enough to trap a tennis ball underneath it, but your eyes are on the target. Both elbows are tucked comfortably against the ribs and the right hand, semi-closed ready to block or hit, is close to the chin. The left hand is held at the same height as the right, but forward of it with about 12" between the gloves. The left glove is closed. Both arms need to feel relaxed, as should the legs. Avoid tension at all costs.

All you need to remember when you first start is:

a   the front foot takes you forwards

b   the back foot takes you backwards

c   if you want to go right push off with the left foot

d   if you want to go left push off with the right foot.

Stay on the balls of the feet and practice maintaining good balance as you move around. Do not bounce; move in a sliding fashion, gliding like a ballroom dancer—a tough ballroom dancer.

2.2 Starting position

a

b

c

d

2.3   Footwork

The left jab

George Foreman always maintained that the jab was the most important punch, and it is always the first punch the novice must master before moving on. It is quite a

2.4   The jab

natural action, more like a spear than a club, delivered sharply and cleanly with instant retraction. Just snap the left glove to the target in a straight line, landing with the knuckle area of the glove. Turn the left hip and shoulder as you do so for added power. The most important part of any punch is the transfer of weight. With the jab you will use the ball of the right foot to propel your weight forward, stepping forward with the left a few inches. The momentum all comes from the ball of the right foot; try to picture somebody standing on your toes as you hit to get the right "feel". Try to hit through the target as opposed to simply reaching it. Retract your glove to the basic stance position in the same plane it travelled forward in, thus avoiding a potential right hand counter being fired through the gap that will be there if you drop the hand. Keep both hands up at all times at this stage of your development.

The straight right (right cross)

This is where you can turn the power on, hitting off your naturally

2.5   The cross

stronger wing, with the satisfying feeling you derive from it. As with the jab you will need the transference of power, driving off the ball of the right foot, turning the hip and shoulder in the direction of the intended target. The upper row of knuckles are the hardest part of

the hand, so attempt to punch slightly downward on impact to ensure it is this part of the hand that makes contact first. Stay upright, keeping the shoulders over the hips, to avoid "reaching" for the target in such a way that the upper body leans forward, which will result in a loss of power, and a swift counter if performed when sparring. When you go forward, your hips must go with you in order to punch your full weight. The left side of the body should allow the right side to pivot, acting like a hinge. Try to punch "through" the target rather than just reaching it. In the meantime, your left hand remains alongside the jaw, providing protection. The elbow should be tucked in tightly to the ribs. Practice on the more static heavy bag to begin with and then graduate to the focus pads. The arm comes back to the defensive position the instant after landing, in exactly the same plane as it made its forward movement, to guard against a counter-attack. Keep your chin down, and your eyes on the target.

The hook

The left hook is more commonly used than the right, usually because it is attempted from the side, to get over, or under, the defensive right hand; trying to hook over the extended left lead is extremely difficult, and the right hook is more commonly a follow-up to a successful left hook, or a body shot (having slipped under a jab).

To launch the hook, shift your weight to the side you intend to hit from, turning the hip and shoulder to that side. Your arm is

2.6   The hook

bent at the elbow, at about 90 degrees. The other hand is pulled close to the head for protection. By rapidly raising the heel and pivoting the hip of the hitting side simultaneously, make a violent (no other word describes the required action) turn and slam the hand against the target with the upper knuckles leading, and the thumb (tucked in tightly) on top at contact. The instant after hitting, whip the hand back to the defensive position. Your feet are in the "20 past 12" position for the jab and the straight right, but for the hook try a minimal change of stance, to "a quarter past 12", in order to allow your hips to turn more easily and rapidly.

The uppercut

This is a punch you would use at close range, almost exclusively used with the strong hand. Try to develop this punch on the "teardrop" type bag (sometimes referred to as the "hook and uppercut" bag). In a "quarter past 12" stance, drop the right shoulder, then drive upwards explosively with the hips as you punch upward in an almost vertical plane. The left

2.7   The uppercut

hand is pulled in to the side of the head to guard against a counter. The punch should travel less than 12" and the hand should return rapidly to the defensive position after contact; do not feel tempted to travel higher than the target, or to start your hand from a low position (you will end up throwing a poor imitation of a "bolo" punch, which would be inadvisable at this stage). Whilst landing the blow your palm should be facing you.

With apologies again to lefthanders, who should reverse all instructions, some combinations to start with are:

left jab, straight right, left hook.

left jab, right uppercut, left hook.

left jab, straight right, left hook, right hook.

There are more punches, usually variations of the above, changing the area of attack or shape of the arm, but don't feel tempted to move on until you have mastered the basic punches.

Making a fist

It is not unusual for beginners to wonder about the best way to "make a fist" in such a way that they will not hurt the hand, especially the thumb. Most injuries that beginners incur are to the wrist (through failure to keep a straight arm on contact), or to the thumb (through incorrect placement of the thumb). The following guide is for the absolute beginner: senior trainers can skip to the next chapter!

1   Settle hand comfortably into glove, pulling hard on the wristband to ensure snug fit. When buying gloves try them on wearing hand-wraps if you intend to train on bags and pads wearing wraps. For this reason (quite apart from the fragrance issue), you need your own bag mitts.

2   Close hand, leaving thumb in the "thumbs up" position (see fig. 2.8).

3   Draw thumb tightly down against fingers (see fig. 2.9).

4   Thumb MUST be retained in this position. Failure to do so will almost certainly lead, eventually, to injury.

5   If this proves problematic, try tailor-made "cut-thumb" style bag mitts, which are generally about the same cost as the orthodox type. A radical alternative would be to cut off the thumb section of your old gloves to see if this provides a solution. As with footwear, never persist with any kit that is uncomfortable. The problem usually just gets worse.

2.8   Thumb up   2.9   The fist

3. Bagwork

According to how well the gym you train in is equipped, you usually have a choice of punchbags. You are advised to wrap your hands (see section on *hand-wrapping*, p. 145), and wear good quality leather bag mitts. Hitting with bare knuckles may look macho, but could put you on the road to arthritic hands in later life.

Light bag

3.1   Left jab on the light bag

Used for fast-punching combinations. It will have a generous swing which encourages changing your angle to avoid the bag and hit it while it is still "on the move". Don't put your hands out to steady it between hits; try to control it as you would an opponent. To stop it dead, hit it hard as it swings directly towards you. Try fast-hitting 2 minute rounds

with a minute break in between. Use "bob and weave" as shown to avoid the bag.

3.2   Bob and weave to avoid the bag

Heavy bag

Build up your punching power with hard, deliberate hitting. Striking this bag as it swings towards you will strengthen the power of your punch. It must be stressed that the arm on hitting must be straight as you make solid contact with the knuckle part of the glove; a cocked wrist can result in wrist injuries when using the heavy bag. Mix up long and close-range punches.

Floor to ceiling ball

Excellent training tool for honing your reflexes. On being struck, the ball whips back and forth proving an extremely elusive moving target, not unlike an opponent

3.3   Straight right on the heavy bag

moving his head rapidly to avoid your punches. This ball can make you look silly at first, as it is hard to judge its unpredictable movement. It teaches a very valuable lesson; if you hit it and then fail to move your head, as you should always do, it comes back

3.4   Floor to ceiling ball

with a vengeance. I once witnessed a spectacular "knockdown" when a guy struck it a massive blow but stayed in the same place with his head fully exposed to the rapid return of the ball. Regular use should improve your accuracy and awareness.

Teardrop bag

Useful to improve hooks and uppercuts, these tend to come with different types of fillings. The maize-filled variety tend to be more stable, but smaller versions are available which call more for speed and accuracy of close-range punches.

Speedball

Teardrop-shaped ball with a wooden platform mounted above. Very good for endurance as you have to keep both hands punching continuously. Also encourages hand and foot co-ordination. Not always popular as punches are made in an unrealistic "rolling" fashion, and the noise they make is incredible. Unsuitable for home use if the walls are thin, or if your neighbours dislike noise.

Wallbags

Sturdy bags, similar to kick-shields used in martial arts (I have seen

3.5 Left hooking the teardrop bag

them used for this purpose) mounted on the wall in a frame or by hooks. In the crowded gyms of Eastern Europe and Cuba they are still quite popular, as they allow more people to train. The drawback is that they are only suitable for straight punches.

Standballs

The standball is an old favourite and although most boxing gyms used to have one they have become something of a rarity, especially due to the fact that they have to be bolted to the floor for safety. They are very good for teaching novices how to jab, and to develop timing.

Hitmen

For a few years now, various figures on a sand or water filled base have become popular for training. The only reason I can see for this is that they are portable, as they cost twice as much as a good quality leather punchbag. They do not, however, need a rafter to hang from for home use. We inherited one at our gym because a guy who trained there was on orders to get rid of it when he moved in with his girlfriend, who hated the sight of it. It was quite warmly received and got a lot of use. It resembled the top half of a tough-looking, well-built muscleman. Unfortunately "he" couldn't take the punches and was decapitated after a few months. Suitable for home training but pricey. Another version lights up when hit—no comment.

Whichever bag you work on, best results come from hitting not just to reach the bag, but to visualise yourself punching right "through" the bag.

Access to punchbags

James Brown, whose version of *Night Train*, incidentally, is excellent training music, may have a brand new bag, but you will need to take several precautions before buying one for the home. If you live in a converted factory space, a solid loft apartment, or own a roomy brick-built shed or garage, or a similarly robust setting, all you need is a stout hook to hang your bag from. This, however, may create certain problems, the most common of which are as follows.

Structural damage. People often fail to recognise the stress engendered by continual sessions on even a light bag. Bringing the ceiling down can prove more costly than gym membership; a risky venture in the average home. If you are tempted to install one, ensure you consult a trusted architect or builder first.

Noise. Your neighbours are unlikely to suffer the constant tattoo and dull thuds rendered by your efforts.

Fittings and fixings can be costly if you have to employ somebody to install it, and unless space is not at a premium you will have a storage problem. Your nearest and dearest might not consider it an attractive feature if constantly on view.

Punchbags can be as inexpensive as £30 for the vinyl variety, or quite costly for a top of the range (like Reyes or Everlast) leather version. For about £90 you can get a decent filled leather bag. Ebay is worth investigating if you are not bothered about a second hand one. The local free newspapers usually advertise plenty just after Christmas as the new owners discover that the well-intentioned gift cannot be hung anywhere at home. It is wisest to buy a filled bag; home filling is never as good as the manufacturer's product. Freestanding punchbags, the base filled with sand or water for stability, are available (for about £200-£250) but you will need a strong floor to withstand the inevitable wear and tear. They are great to use as they make 360° movement possible.

3.6   Freestanding punchbag

4.   Focus pad training

Focus pads

Focus pads allow for a range of shots. Every punch can be attempted, especially with an adept pad-holder. Pad holding is a specific skill and can improve the holder's reflexes and footwork as well as those of the hitter. In advanced drills (see *pad drills*, p. 30), it can improve stamina, endurance and motor skills. They are excellent, some might say irreplaceable, for coaches to illustrate the correct punching technique and develop combination punching.

(See also section on *equipment* p. 136.)

4.1   Focus pads held for left jab, right cross

Focus mitts

Focus mitts, also known as coaching mitts, resemble a huge sparring glove, with heavy padding and a focus area on the palm. They take pad holding a stage further, allowing the instructor to hold a more demanding session by switching from holding to hitting, testing defensive and counter-punching capabilities.

4.2   Focus mitts

How to hold

4.3   Focus pads held for a) left jab b) right cross c) right cross, left hook

Holding the pads needs to be taught initially, to help prevention of elbow ligament injuries, such as the dreaded tennis elbow (above the elbow), or golfer's elbow (below the elbow), which can be suffered without ever hefting a racquet or club.

The arms should be relaxed to alleviate the "shock factor". The holder must learn to anticipate blows and to absorb their energy in a technique similar to fielding a cricket ball, by using a little "give" on contact. Reduce risk of eye injury by securing flappy straps before use.

To help prevent strains and overuse injuries, pre-stretch the forearm as illustrated in fig. 4.4. After a hard session on the pads repeat the stretches and shake your arms and fingers out.

4.4 Stretches

Combinations on the focus pads

If you are starting out, spend a little time just practising a basic jab and cross combination to get the correct range, footwork and "feel" for the pads.

Progress to adding hooks and uppercuts, both of which need professional tuition to produce good, safe technique.

Here are some suggested combinations; apologies to left-handers, who will have to adapt all instructions to suit a right lead.

Where the terms "head" and "body" are used, this refers to height and position of pad with reference to these targets.

4.5	Jab	Cross	Left hook	Right hook
4.6	Jab	Jab	Cross	Left hook
4.7	Left hook to body	Left hook to head	Right uppercut	
4.8	Jab	Cross	Left hook	Right uppercut
4.9	Jab to body	Cross to head	Left hook to body	
4.10	Jab	Cross	Left uppercut	Right uppercut
4.11	Jab to head	Cross to body	Left hook to head	Right cross to body
4.12	Left jab	Left hook	Right cross	
4.13	Jab high and low, holder moving side to side, backward and forward			
4.14	Left hook high	Right hook high	Left hook low	Right hook low
4.15	Holder keeps pads moving; attempt to jab both pads			

4.16 Using bob and weave technique, duck incoming hooks and reply with hooks from both hands

4.17   Jabs with pads held "short and long", followed by "long and short"

4.18   Using "swayback / snapback" technique, avoid right cross, counter with left hook, right uppercut, left jab

4.19   Block incoming jab and counter with own jab; block incoming right with
        shoulder roll and counter with own cross

5. Specific Boxing Drills

1. Heavy hands

Improves hand-speed and power. You can buy purpose-built gloves for this (expensive option), or try these cheaper options:

2 × 1kg dumbbells

2 × smooth stones of reasonable size and weight to fit in the palm.

I was fascinated (and impressed) to see somebody using a couple of alabaster eggs— perfect hand-fit and perfect weight!

Shadow-box holding the weights for a set number of rounds, then discard and shadow-box the same number with empty hands, concentrating on hand-speed.

5.1 Shadowbox with hand weights

2. Box jumps

Improves ankle joint strength, improves push-off from rear foot which is essential in punching, especially regarding jabs and straight punches.

You will need a step box, similar to the Reebok version, which must be sturdy and stable, placed on a firm surface.

Beginner level using 1 box

Start by standing alongside box. Jump sideways, two-footed onto box,

5.2   Box jumps: advanced level

then off the other side to land two-footed. Continue jumping from side to side, taking two bounces on the box and on landing.

Intermediate level using 1 box

As beginner, but now taking only one bounce on the box. Graduate to taking a single bounce on landing as well.

Advanced level using 1 or more boxes

Clear the box completely with a two-footed jump from side to side. Once competent try with 2 or more boxes, clearing each individual box without landing on it. Leave about 2 foot between the boxes. At this and the highly advanced stage, the intention is to develop explosive lateral power.

training tip

Be patient, and satisfy yourself with short periods, such as half a minute to start with, building up in 10-second increments, until you can last for 3 minutes—your ultimate target. When you jump, perform a sweeping upward motion of the arms, raising your hands forward to level with your shoulders. I recommend wearing running shoes with heel support for minimum discomfort to calf area.

Highly advanced (killer) level; using 5 boxes and one "motivator"

The motivator faces the jumper and then moves laterally, changing direction frequently and abruptly. The jumper has to "mirror" the lateral movement, clearing the boxes as the motivator does. Masochists can do this with hand-weights.

3.   Tennis ball drill

Shadow box with a tennis ball held in place under the chin in order to adopt the correct head position; very small folk can use a golf ball. Try working on punchbag keeping the ball in place, then let the ball drop but retain the same head position.

(see also *solo training workout*, p. 102)

6.   Skipping

There are a number of reasons why you should make skipping an essential part of your training regime.

1   Improves co-ordination. Skipping gets upper and lower body to co-ordinate movements (a crucial factor in boxing).

2   Allows aerobic and anaerobic training. You (or your instructor) make the choice of what level of exertion to train at.

3   Increases joint strength, and, as in most rebounding exercises, improves bone density.

4   Increases leg power and endurance.

5   Tones muscle and reduces fat.

6   Beneficial even when used in short periods. If you intend to box for 3 minute rounds then intensive skipping in 3 minute bursts, with short rests in between, makes sense.

Considerations are:

length, material and quality of rope

surface

footwear.

Ropes

There are numerous different types of ropes but, for training, I would recommend a leather rope, a PVC speed rope or a heavy rope composed of beads or rubber or plastic tubing. With all ropes get them properly sized (fig. 6.1). Most starters need a rope they can stand on with the leading foot where the handles reach the armpits. Extremely tall people may

6.1 Sizing the rope

need to get a "made to measure". Ropes can easily be reduced in length for shorter people. A medium-thickness leather rope with ball-bearing handles is, I have found, the easiest rope for most people to learn with.

Leather ropes

Traditionally the boxing training choice, good enough for Ali and both "Sugar Rays" (Robinson and Leonard), so good enough for anybody. Affordable, although some have swivelling or ball-bearing handles and work out a little more expensive.

PVC speed ropes

As the name implies these fast-turning ropes are intended to improve foot speed, and are, like leather ropes, modestly priced.

If you are trying one for the first time my tip would be to wear jogging bottoms, to minimise "whiplash" until you become accustomed to the rope.

Heavy ropes

Help to strengthen arms and upper body. Should only be used in short bursts of 2-3 minutes to avoid excessive strain.

Surface

Do not skip on concrete, tarmac or other equally hard surfaces. The very least you will suffer is sore calf muscles. Ideally you need a sprung wooden floor or a rubberised gym floor. Skipping indoors on a carpeted floor is unlikely to prove harmful.

Footwear

Running or tennis shoes, cross-training shoes, boxing or wrestling boots are all ideal. Make sure your laces are securely tightened. If you feel the desire to skip in bare feet, use a judo mat or a carpeted floor.

Other considerations

Long hair? Pin it down.

Loose-fitting spectacles? Tie them around back of head.

Ladies are advised to a) get a good sports bra b) "spend a penny" before commencing (you'll have to trust my judgement on this one; I don't wish to go into pelvic floors and internal plumbing details here).

Actually getting started!

Before you start, you are going to have to tell yourself that this will require a little patience. I have taught some people to skip in 20 seconds and others have taken months to become even moderately happy with their results. Mercifully, these are in the minority as most people with any sort of sports, dance or gym background usually pick it up in minutes.

Where possible, stand opposite a full-length mirror. You need to keep your head up at all times. To maintain a good ergonomic position, resist the temptation to look down at your feet to see how they're doing!

Get the rope to rest on the back of your knees, keep arms and legs loose and relaxed and start to bounce lightly with feet a few inches apart—no rope yet! Once you have established an easy, effortless bouncing rhythm, bring the rope over your head, clearing your feet with each revolution. You will hit your feet from time to time, which is frustrating just as you think you are getting the hang of it. A good tip is that when this happens, don't stop bouncing; just flip the rope over your head back to the start-up

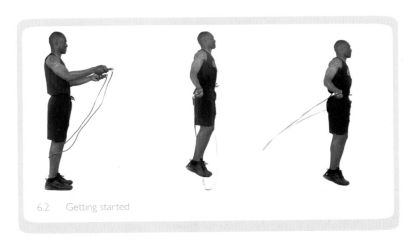
6.2   Getting started

position and then bring the rope back in. This will not only help to improve your technique, but it will save interrupting a continuous workout. Again, be patient. Remember when you first learned to cycle and drive; this is simple by comparison.

Once you have grasped the basics, improvement will only come by regular practice. Do not despair if success is not instant; I have not had a single failure in the hundreds I have taught, no matter how uncoordinated or unfit they were.

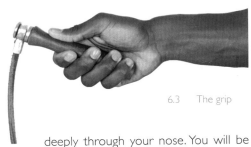
6.3   The grip

Breathe in quite deeply through your nose. You will be surprised how tiring skipping is initially. Gradually bring the elbows in closer to the ribs and experiment with different grips; try extending the thumb along the handle. After your first couple of minutes stop to stretch your calf muscle and Achilles for about 10 seconds before re-starting; these areas take a pounding during skipping (see section on *stretching*, p. 124). For this reason I generally advise starting in running shoes with cushioned heels (with gel, air capsules or waffles in the heels).

Advanced techniques (but not too advanced!)

Alternate stepping

Start out in the two-footed bounce and then alternately place a foot in front, as if putting out a couple of lighted cigarette butts! Vary this by taking a double beat with each foot.

6.4   Alternate stepping

6.5   Ski hops

Ski hops

Feet together, hop from side to side then switch to hopping backward and forward.

Split steps

As you skip, start with feet together, then open to shoulder width and back again.

6.6   Split steps

6.7   Hop and kick

Hop and kick

Hop on one foot and take a small kick to the front—the classic-looking "boxer's skip".

6.8   Leg raise

Leg raise

Work the lower abs as you skip! While bouncing on one foot raise the other leg until it is bent at a right angle.

Bumps

Finish a work-out off by jumping as the rope spins twice (fig. 6.11). See how many you can do, note it, then attempt to beat your own personal best.

Cross-overs

You will need a longish rope and the longer the handles all the better. Start off bouncing then cross your arms in front of you so the rope forms a loop which you pass under your feet with a downward sweep of your crossed arms. Once the rope has flipped under your feet bring your arms back to the start position. At first

6.9   Crossovers

6.10   Running in place

it will take a little getting used to but think how impressive it will look once you can perform a continuous series of cross-overs, *a la* Sugar Ray Leonard.

Running in place

Run on the spot as you skip, varying the pace but finishing on a flat-out burst. If you have a good space, jog forward and backward, or create your own variations on the running theme.

Back and forth

Run forward for a few yards, then back up with alternating backwards steps. Alternatively, go forwards and backwards with alternate steps, varying the speeds and stride patterns.

training tip

Skipping to music alleviates boredom and, given the appropriate music, helps the sense of rhythm. Leonard Cohen and Wagner are inadvisable; pick your own upbeat favourites ensuring other gym users do not object. Not everybody may share your love of hip-hop, trance etc.

Skipping backwards

The ultimate skip challenge! Start with the rope resting on your shins and try skipping by taking the rope back over your head in the reverse direction. This takes quite a lot of getting used to!

6.11 Bumps

7.   Running

Running benefits both aerobic and anaerobic capacity, according to the intensity applied. Long continuous running, at a pace at which you can converse with a partner, will give you an adequate reservoir of stamina. Aim at two or more sessions a week, remembering that, at worst, one is better than none.

If you are starting out, or have not run since you were forced to at school sports, try the following approach.

1   Walk briskly for 3-5 minutes.

2   Jog easily for 3-5 minutes.

3   Stop for a short stretch. Stretch legs: quads, hamstrings, calves and Achilles. Do not stretch hard or deep as this is a light, cursory pre-run stretch. Perform all stretches from a standing position; you are not warm enough yet to lay down for any of them (see section on *stretching*, p. 124).

4   Look at your watch and note the time. Run for 7-8 minutes, turn round and run back to start area, tapering off to a very slow pace over the last few hundred metres, slowing to a walk. Walk for 3-5 minutes to cool down, breathing deeply to recover.

5   Shake limbs out to loosen them. Stretch each body part for 30 seconds each, lying down if possible (if there is a clean, dry comfortable surface available). If you have returned home from your run, enjoy a luxurious stretch on the carpet, after checking you don't have mud spattered up your back; I have found that this is not too well received.

Check how you felt after your initial 15 minute run. If you felt nauseous, exhausted or full of aches and pains, then it will be best to stick to 15 minute runs until such time as you feel fine after the run. Once you can run with a degree of comfort over this period it is time to move up. Take a couple of days off from running after a session, but not your other training. You should have recovered completely when the time comes to have another run.

Moving up

Get your watch on and, using the earlier procedure, progress to doing 20 and then 30 minute runs: the ideal distance. Use the car speedo to see how far you have run or memorise the landmarks if you run in a park. Try to improve your times. If you want to check on your fitness level, take your pulse at the completion of the run or try wearing a heart rate monitor.

When you have mastered a steady 30-minute run, try, once a week, varying the speed by speeding up for short intervals, alternating with easy-pace running.

Running kit

Shoes

Running requires running shoes, preferably purchased from a recommended, good quality running shop, such as *Runners Need, Run and Become* or another specialist outlet. Try not to scrimp on shoes; you will be glad you didn't. You may have to travel a few miles to find a specialist running shop but, as opposed to the assorted injuries that lie in wait for cheap or unsuitable fashion shoes, this is a small price to pay. Most of the reputable shops advertise in such magazines as *Runner* and *Runner's World*; these magazines also test and make recommendations on shoes and give some great tips on all aspects of running. While getting your shoes, pick up some running socks. You will notice the difference from ordinary socks in the comfort of the fit.

The shop assistant, when fitting you for shoes, will get you to run on a treadmill and video you to see what kind of style you have. He or she will probably tell you that you pronate, supinate or are "normal"; whichever they detect will govern their choice of the correct shoe for you. This doesn't happen in "fashion" sports outlets, where appearance and price are the priorities. Some shoes use gel in the heels or forefoot, others have air capsules or "waffles". Whichever you choose, they should feel great once you take your first run in them.

It used to be common to get boxers to run in heavy boots, but I feel that whilst this is excellent for the military (who will have to run in boots), comfortable, user-friendly shoes and socks (not nylon: cotton or specialist socks work best) will save you from the heroics of running with blisters.

It should not be assumed, however, that even the best running shoes in the world will save you from injuries if there is an underlying problem. If you find you are suffering from strains and minor pulls, try contacting a specialist in sports injuries before things get too serious and you are laid off with an injury.

Clothing

If you are unsure of the weather (which even the weather forecasters are in Britain), dress up rather than down. A hat can be carried or stuffed into a pocket if you get too hot, and a long-sleeved top can be tied about the waist. In winter a hat is needed to stop body heat escaping from the top of the head.

Thin waterproofs are a good investment. They will not only protect you from the wet but from the wind as well. There are some great running garments available that will keep you warm, cool or wick away sweat as desired. You can find them in running magazines for mail order, in shops, or on the web.

Steer well clear of bin-liners or other such "aids" to lose weight, or leg-weights to build leg strength. The former can do you harm by causing dehydration; the latter spoil your natural running rhythm.

Timing and running sensibly

If you have the constraints of full-time employment (as most people still have) or shift-work, you can only run when you can spare the time. However, it makes very little difference at what time you run. It is a fallacy that running early in the morning will burn fat faster due to the lack of carbohydrate; tests have proved this to be false[1]. Try to eat a bowl of cereal before running: it is usually easy to digest for most people and will give you enough energy for your 20-30 minute run[2]. Running in the early evening before your meal makes sound sense. Your limbs are nicely warmed up by this time of day, unlike your "early-bird" counterpart, who may still feel a little stiff after rising. Evening running in summer also means avoiding the midday sun and becoming overheated.

Running safely

At the time of writing, in London, where we train, female joggers or runners (who have often been a source of merriment for the moronic element of society) have actually been, on at least two occasions, victims of vicious assaults, one such incident tragically resulting in the murder of a young American jogger. It is an extremely sad indictment of our society that women runners—and in some urban areas after dark, male runners—need extra vigilance. It is always better to err on the side of caution, and I advise the following for maximising your safety:

Women who run in any area in which they feel unsafe or are advised to be aware, should ideally find a running partner or partners, there

---

[1] Brian Sharkey *Fitness and Health*

[2] Nancy Clarke *Sports Nutrition Guidebook*

See also *helpful literature, p. 160*

being more strength in numbers. Try, however, to stick to populated, well-lit areas.

Leave the walkman at home, if there is traffic or you know the area has a dubious reputation. I have spoken to more than one person who has suffered being mugged through inattention caused by having a walkman playing. They did not hear the approach of their attackers, who were obviously aware of this fact.

Wear reflective materials at night.

Run in well-lit areas at night (I once missed the edge of the kerb in the dark and sprained my ankle, and therefore speak from sad experience; I have not run in bad lighting since).

Distance

The longest distance you need to run is 10-12 miles, and if so only once a week. More distance would not be helpful; a 3 mile run 2-3 times a week will be a great maintenance distance.

Treadmills

I have divided my arguments on these into "for" and "against"; in my experience some love them, some hate them or, like myself, only use them out of necessity. It must be said, however, that many people who get a decent level of fitness from them would not venture to run outside, and will probably only ever run on a treadmill because that is where they feel comfortable.

7.1   Light, pre-run stretch

For and against

Fine when weather is snowy, stormy or otherwise foul.

If you feel a slight strain, you are not stranded miles from anywhere.

Recoverers from injury can give themselves a fitness check in a warm, safe environment.

Most modern treadmills monitor time, calories and pulse. They have miles or kilometres readouts to save mathematical gymnastics.

For beginners it can help to build confidence before "hitting the road".

Can be elevated for hill running. The lowest incline setting is suited to the faster runner right from the start of their run.

You can wear a walkman, discman, iPod or whatever in safety and, on most treadmills, store a drinks bottle easily to hand.

You have to stay on the pace, or finish up flying off the back (I have witnessed this twice; in both cases people did not operate the controls properly).

There is no getting away from the unpleasant fact that some individuals sweat all over the treadmill and don't always mop up. If you have a tendency to perspire copiously, take a towel on board.

You will tend to run in a stride pattern that suits treadmill running. It will differ from your natural technique.

Other users get twitchy if there is a limited number of machines. Some clubs limit use to 20 minutes.

People have been known to make spectacular exits from treadmills, usually through looking at a TV monitor while increasing speed. I once saw a guy draped across a nearby pec-deck machine making this very manoeuvre. They must be treated with respect to ensure safety. Read any applicable safety warnings posted by the machine.

Some clubs, in the interests of safety, govern the speed quite drastically, inhibiting the faster runner.

AGAINST

Interval training

Teaches your body to cope with high intensity work by interspersing anaerobic training with short recovery intervals. It is not the most popular form of training, as you will need to be completely exhausted at the end of each interval. It is extremely hard work but does get results, giving you the potential of improving both aerobic and anaerobic capacity. Anaerobic capacity is improved on runs that force you to use up all your oxygen (oxygen debt), and cause a lactic build-up that your cardio system will be forced to adapt to.

There are many schedules to utilise interval running, but here is a simple and usable example to start with. Progress can be charted, in this case, by a partner with a stop-watch who can see if your times improve. Take your pulse as you recover to act as a guide to improved cardiovascular fitness, or wear a heart-rate monitor.

Interval training example

Start by running 50 metres (graduate by 10-metre increments to 100, 200 and 400 metres). Select a distance that has permanent features or markings, for example two lamp-posts or trees in a park the required distance apart. Warm up first with a jog, long enough to warm your muscles (this will depend on temperature and body type), then have a short stretch. You then sprint the required distance as fast as possible. On completion, walk back to your mark, regaining your breath ready for the next interval. Repeat this procedure for a set number of intervals, perhaps 10 to start with. As you adapt to this training, increase the distance and the effort expounded. Try not to overdo it at first; aim for gradual, steady improvement.

Fartlek

This excellent training system is not as popular as it should be, mostly due to its almost quaintly vulgar name. I am informed that it is Swedish for "speed-play", which is how it would have been better introduced to gain respectability.

It employs varied pace running. An easy example is the widely-used football training drill in which the squad run at an easy pace but the back marker or markers must always sprint to the front of the squad. Fartlek can be structured beforehand to be run in a formal pattern of intervals of jogging, hard-running and walking, or just feel free to do as you please while out running alone or with friends. As with your continuous runs, aim for a 30 minute session.

Surfaces

If you are just starting out, look for parkland with firm grass or sandy paths as user-friendly surfaces. If you have, or have had, knee problems, these are definitely the surfaces for you, at least initially. Sandy beaches look inviting and have an inviting environment, but are only good if they have hard-packed sand; soft sand pulls hard on the Achilles tendon. The worst surface, unfortunately, is the most common and most available: pavement. While "roadwork" is the term often applied to the running aspect of boxing training, if you have not run distance before or have not been running recently you may do well to seek an alternative, kinder surface than a stone pavement. Seasoned runners simply get used to pavement running and learn to adapt, usually from necessity. If you live in an area where they have tarmac pavements, or the cable layers have, unintentionally, recently left a ready-made soft tarmac path, count yourself fortunate; tarmac is a great surface to run on. I would advise against running distances on astroturf. An osteopath informed me that God invented astroturf to help his profession prosper; it can play havoc with hamstrings in particular.

8. Weight Training

Weight training is an invaluable tool for boxing in that it:

builds strength

improves muscular fitness

burns off excess fat (more than most people realise)

retards osteoporosis (especially in women).

Years ago, weight training was discouraged as an element of boxing training. It was thought by many coaches to make you "muscle-bound" and hence cumbersome.

To achieve positive improvements, you really need to train twice a week. Try to dovetail your workouts in such a way that they do not interfere with your specific boxing training sessions.

A system I have found successful is to train twice a week, using two differing workouts:

an all-body workout for overall maintenance, training all muscle groups

a workout using only the big muscle groups worked very hard. Most people find once a week is enough for this workout! I refer to this as the "hard-gainer workout".

The choice for your actual training will now be between machines or free weights, or a combination of both. Both have arguments for and against, but if you are a newcomer to weight training then I would advise machines. There is no point in training with equipment you patently dislike; speak to a qualified instructor who should find something to suit you.

For and against machine weights

Restrict movement to a single, and not always natural, plane.

Inhibit motor skills: moves can be performed in robotic manner.

Expensive: most people could not afford to have a comprehensive set at home.

Require maintenance.

AGAINST

FOR

Safer (with professional instruction).

Practically eliminate theft.

User-friendly for beginners.

For most exercises, time saving.

For and against free weights

Require specific professional instruction for safe use, unlike machines.

Prone to misuse. People do not always replace weights in the rack after use, which they should to prevent accidents happening.

Thefts are not unknown.

More time-consuming. You have to change plates or wait for another user to free up particular weights.

AGAINST

FOR

Versatile.

Suit advanced trainers.

Encourage motor skills and bilateral strength (with use of dumbbells).

Cheaper (most people can afford a full set of free weights for use in the garage, shed, spare room or wherever, allowing home training).

When all aspects are considered, it is up to the individual as to which mode they prefer. Don't be a free weights "snob", looking disparagingly at machine trainers. There should be no elitism in weight training, and it is unfortunate that there often is.

The routines I prescribe can be performed with machines, free weights or a combination of both.

The workouts

All-body workout

This is designed as a 10 repetition max. workout, whereby the first repetition is easy but by the tenth repetition it becomes fairly demanding.

8.1   Flyes or pec-deck (chest)

8.2   Bench press (chest)

8.3   Single arm rows (or lat pull downs on machine) (lats)

8.4   Upright rows using barbell (or cable station) (trapezius)

8.5   Front raise (front of shoulders)

8.6   Shoulder press with barbell, dumbbells or machine (middle of shoulders)

8.7   Seated bent-over lateral raise (rear of shoulders)

8.8   Bicep curls using machine, barbells or dumbbells (bicep)

8.9   Leg extension on machine (quads)

8.10 Squats with barbell (quads, hamstrings and glutes) or leg curls on machine (hamstrings)

8.11 Tricep pushdowns on cable station or seated dumbell tricep extensions (tricep)

Do 3 sets of 10 repetitions, working slowly on all exercises.

Rest for 30 seconds between sets, but before starting each new discipline do a set of 10-20 abdominal exercises (see *core training*, p.78, for exercises).

training tip

Before workout, warm-up 5 minutes; short stretch 6-8 seconds each muscle group.

After workout, cooldown 5 minutes; long stretch, at least 30 seconds each body part.

Hard-gainers workout (advanced trainers only!)–The 6x6

This is a very demanding workout. I must stress that anyone attempting it should be fit and have been weight training regularly for some months before embarking on it. Rest 2 minutes between each set (no abs work, just rest!). Sip water between sets. A training partner would be of significant benefit, primarily to "spot", but also to encourage each other.

warm-up–10 minutes aerobic

pre-stretch–6-8 seconds per body part.

1 set of 15 reps using only the bar (this is to "warm up"), followed by 6 sets of 6 repetitions.

This should be performed with as heavy a weight as you can manage for the 6 repetitions.

You will need a "spotter" or alternatively use machine.

HG1   Bench press (see fig. 8.2)

1 set of 15 repetitions using a low setting to warm up. If performed with free weights by doing single arm rows, use a light dumbell to warm up.

Using the "v" grip attachment on the lat-pulldown machine, 6 sets of 6 repetitions as heavy as you can manage for the 6 repetitions.

Alternatively, 6 sets of 6 repetitions of single arm rows with as heavy a dumbbell as you can manage for 6 repetitions.

HG2   V grip pulldowns or single arm rows (see fig. 8.3)

Can be performed with barbell, dumbbells, in squat rack, or using Smith machine.

Start with 1 set of 15 repetitions using no weights, to warm up.

Perform 6 sets of 6 repetitions using as much weight as you can manage for the 6 repetitions.

HG3   Squats (see fig. 8.10)

Can only be performed authentically with a barbell to achieve the desired action and results. If you are not totally confident of your deadlift technique you must get assistance from a qualified instructor.

Warm up by performing deadlift manoeuvre without weight.

Follow with 6 sets of 6 repetitions with as heavy a weight as you can manage.

HG4   Deadlifts

cooldown–10 minutes aerobic

post-exercise stretch–minimum 30 seconds per body part

(see section on *flexibility and stretching* p. 124).

Summary of 6x6 (Free Weights)

Warm up, pre-stretch 5-6 seconds	5 mins
Bench press	6 sets × 6 reps
Single arm rows	6 sets × 6 reps
Squats	6 sets × 6 reps
Deadlifts	6 sets × 6 reps
Cool down, post stretch 30 seconds	5-10 mins

If you are even moderately unsure of your technique on any of these exercises, due to the effort you will expend don't be too proud to get an instructor to help you perfect your technique.

All your exercises must be performed slowly and with full control, using the full range of motion. Take 2-3 seconds to lift the weight, pause for 1-2 seconds, then take 2-3 seconds to lower weight.

This routine should only be performed once a week, and then only for a limited number of months before changing. It pays to change your routine at regular intervals as when your body becomes adept at working in a certain exercise pattern there is a tendency to plateau when you stop making positive progress in strength gains.

Make sure that 2-3 hours before you train, you drink a couple of glasses of water and try to eat a high carbohydrate meal or snack. If you are at work and this is inconvenient, try to get hold of some fruit or yoghurt. A sandwich with a protein filling (fish, egg, or cheese, for example) would be better than nothing. If you have experienced fatigue during training, grab a bottle of sports drink, such as Lucozade or Isostar, and "top up" during your workout. I realise that hard-working people do not have the luxury of sitting down to a nutritionally balanced meal as prescribed by their personal trainer.

After your workout you will need to refuel. Again, if you are dashing back to work, or have to catch the train, you will need to pick up something ready-made. Go for fruit, milk, one of the many "smoothie" drinks available, yoghurt, a sports bar. When shopping, pick up a multi-pack of raisins in small boxes; throw one or two into your bag when you pack your kit.

Try to eat within two hours after your workout; failure to eat at all is like asking a builder to extend your property by supplying the plans but no materials.

If you have got home fairly late, eat a light meal, for example salad with lean meat or sardines, pasta with a tomato-based sauce, a tin of soup, or a jacket potato.

The next day aim to incorporate a more aerobic-based workout, which should, after a little initial stiffness, loosen you up.

This workout will not suit everybody, and takes quite a lot of adherence. Some people I have put on it have sworn by it, and still do in many cases. Others have detested it and given up on it after a short period. Like all training, you will not know how much you are willing to extend yourself until you actually try. Do not be put off by other users lifting much heavier weights than you; you are not competing with them and this is only one element of your varied training regime, whereas weight-training is probably all they ever do. Be happy with your own gains, no matter how small: you *are* making an improvement.

Progress

The principle that is generally held, regarding weight training benefits, is that doing an all-body workout (as in the examples here) will respond to these frequencies:

once a week = maintenance

twice a week = maintenance and some progress

three times a week = progress.

The above are all dependent on how much effort and weight you are prepared to use!

Try to avoid weight training and cardio work on the same day. If, due to commitments, you have no alternative, and simply *have* to do them on the same day, then:

do the weights *first*

keep the aerobic/cardio work light.

Women and weights

The same goes for the ladies. With more and more women taking up boxing training, weight training will give you both strength and tone, and—please trust me here—without the bulk! It will improve your bone density and reduce the risk of osteoporosis. This has been proven in scientific tests and trials to be indisputably true. Due to possessing only small amounts of testosterone (the male sex hormone, which helps men put on muscle), women cannot develop huge, masculine-looking muscles. Women competing in martial arts such as wrestling, judo and Vale Tudo who I have trained have made enormous strength gains, but while their muscles have become clearly defined they have never taken on a "manly" look.

As for Cro-magnon types who look down their nose at women working out with weights, treat them with the contempt they deserve. A weights area should be free of discrimination of any form; in my experience most intelligent guys enjoy having women around the gym. I tend to worry about men who only enjoy "stag" company and don't like gyms that encourage women. If you have never used weights before, ladies, then give it a go. Make sure you have a qualified instructor with whom you feel comfortable; if not, get a new one. You do not want to pay for something less than the standard you expect.

Weight training programme

			Machine/ dumbells?	Sets	P
1	Warm up–5 minutes aerobic				
2	Stretches–6-8 seconds each				
3	Exercises:				
	Pecs				
	Bench press				
	Single arm rows/ lat pulldowns				
	Upright rows				
	Front raise				
	Shoulder press				
	Seated bent over lateral raise				
	Leg extension				
	Leg curls / Squats				
	Bicep curls				
	Tricep pushdowns				
	Hard gainers–Bench press				
	Hard gainers–V grip pulldown				
	Hard gainers–Squats				
	Hard gainers–Deadlifts				
4	Cooldown–5 minutes aerobic				
5	Cooldown stretches–30 seconds each				

Photocopiable page © Ian Oliver 2004

Weights	1	2	3	4	5	6	7

9.   Calisthenics

Don't worry if you are unfamiliar with the term; it simply refers to body resistance exercise, usually called calisthenics in the USA. Unbelievably, considering the dependence martial arts, boxing and the military have on it, it is derived from the Greek words "kallos" (beauty) and "sthenos" (strength). For now we are going to skip the beauty part and home in on the strength element.

Why calisthenics? Two reasons:

it's cheap

it's convenient.

Exercises

9.1   Push ups

Push/press ups

Easy to explain, but, as all former schoolboys remember, hard to perform in a large number of repetitions. Keep body straight and start with hands under shoulders. Variations involve narrowing or widening hand positions or putting feet up, such as on a box. Primarily they work the chest, the front of the shoulders and the triceps. For additional benefit, and of course difficulty, raise the feet on a box or ball (see fig. 10.2, p. 80).

9.2 Curl ups

Curl-ups

Straight-leg sit-ups became taboo a few years ago, but have made a bit of a comeback with hardcore trainers lately. Play safe and stick to bent-leg curl-ups, raising just the shoulder blades off the floor as your upper body curls forward. Do not pull on the head or neck, and try to contract the abdominal muscles as you perform the move. Do not hold your breath.

Reverse curls

Lie on your back with hands close to your sides. Your legs should be bent at the knee to form a right-angle or straight with the soles of your feet facing the ceiling. From this position slowly lift your backside off the floor by bringing your legs toward your ribs. Once your backside is off the floor lower it back to start position. Take it slowly and try to contract your abs while breathing naturally.

9.3 Reverse curls

Crunches

Starting in the bent-knee position as in the reverse curls, bring your head towards your knees by lifting your shoulder blades off the floor. At the same time, lift your backside off the floor to bring your knees towards your ribs. Perform slowly, concentrating on control of movement.

(see also *core training*, p.78 for more abs exercises).

9.4   Crunches

Tricep dips

Use a sturdy box or chair. Place hands behind you, with the heel of each hand firmly gripping the edge of the surface. Keeping the legs straight makes this a little harder; try it with bent legs first. Let your arms form a right-angle on each repetition.

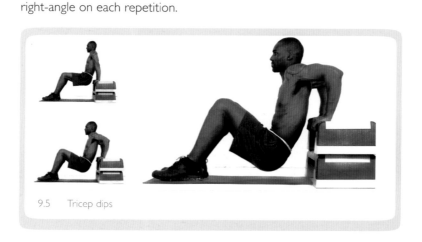

9.5   Tricep dips

9.6   Chin-ups

Chin-ups (also called pull-ups)

If you can find a suitably low bar you can do an easier modified version of this exercise; if you can't, you'll just have to go for the full-on chin-ups. An exercise that suits featherweights more than heavyweights, it involves grasping an overhead bar with a wide overhand grip and then pulling yourself high enough to look over the bar (you do not need to actually get your chin over it, despite the name of the exercise). It is primarily a back exercise, working the lats, trapezius, teres and rhomboids, but it is in the biceps you will feel the effect, according to how much body weight you have!

Back extensions

Lie face down on a comfortable surface; if it's not comfortable to start with it's hardly likely to improve after 10 repetitions. Place your hands lightly on each side of your head and slowly lift your trunk off the floor in a controlled movement. Don't overextend your back. Start with 10-15 repetitions.

9.7   Back extensions

9.8   Step ups

Step-ups

If you do not have a Reebok-type step box, or even a sturdy milk crate then use the bottom stair. Either alternate lead foot or start with 10 on one side and then switch to the other foot.

To make it harder, carry handweights or a backpack.

Squats

Performed as in weight training but still a decent weight-free exercise, and if you have not performed this exercise with weights previously, a good introduction to an excellent exercise for leg strength and endurance. Build up the number of repetitions to improve endurance.

9.9   Squats

Calf raise

Stand on the bottom stair or a sturdy box with only the toes making contact, supporting yourself with a handrail or by pressing hands against a wall. Allow the heels to descend slowly. Bring the heels back up and rise up fully on your toes. Keep body upright at all stages of the raise. Start with 10 repetitions.

9.10   Calf raise

Hanging leg raise

Grasp an overhead bar with an overhand grip, arms shoulder-width apart. Bend your knees and pull your legs up towards your ribs. The hardest part is to control excess movement to stop your body swinging back and forth. This exercise primarily works the abdominal muscles and the hip flexors.

Lunges

Like squats, usually performed with weights as a strength exercise. Without weights it is particularly beneficial for developing balance and co-ordination, combined with an endurance factor. Start with feet shoulder-width apart. Keeping upper body upright, step forward with one foot, bending the knee to form a right angle, with the lower part of the leg vertical, the knee above the ankle (never beyond it). The rear leg should also form a right angle, the lower section a few inches above the floor. Bring leading leg back and step forward with the other foot, again the legs forming two right angles. Start with 10 repetitions on each leg, building up endurance by increasing the number of repetitions. If you feel wobbly when you first start, try spreading your arms out to the side, like a tightrope walker. Keep your head up at all times to maintain good alignment. If it is possible, check your position in a mirror to help correct form.

9.11 Lunges

10. Core training for boxing

Strong abs are an essential for boxing. A powerful mid-section provides a powerful base to give stability when balance is threatened by demanding movements, both those that you make voluntarily, and those forced upon you by external factors.

What is required is a strong but flexible core, the term for the deep abdominal and spinal muscles supporting your spine. Concentrate on building this "stabilising belt", and make the physical outward appearance of a secondary nature; too much emphasis is placed on working toward the chiselled, "ice-cube tray" look. If your abs look great, consider it a bonus; what you need them for is to support you efficiently and effortlessly throughout a high-impact sport.

Don't forget that if you are working your abs hard, you must not neglect your back. Combine "crunch" sessions with back extensions and dorsal raises. Abs exercises should form only part of your core training.

While there are more items of equipment I could name, the ones I have selected are:

1   the exercise ball
2   the medicine ball (both types—bouncy and non-bouncy)
3   the power wheel.

The exercise ball

Also known as the "Swiss ball", the "stability ball" and the "medi-ball". At our gym some of the less strait-laced weight-trainers have other names for it, but none of them are repeatable here.

It was first introduced by remedial therapists to assist primarily with back problems, and was greeted with a mixture of curiosity and derision on its early appearance in many gyms. It is fair to say that it has become popular due to the variation of exercises it allows. You use numerous muscles just to prevent yourself from falling off it! A physio I know uses one instead of a chair in his office.

The extra effort required to manage the additional element of instability allows for increased strength gains. It takes a little getting used to; start out on a soft surface just to be safe.

It encourages the body to work as a single unit in an effort to maintain balance, while performing tasks in what would be an otherwise wobbly environment. Most importantly, apart from helping to improve balance and motor skills, it is a tool to improve your core strength in those all-important deep-lying muscles. A bonus is that you can use it instead of a bench for home training.

Recommended exercises

10.1   Wall squat (with or without handweights)

10.2 Push ups a) with hands on ball b) with feet on ball

10.3 Curls a) fingers touching head b) holding medicine ball

10.4 Back extensions

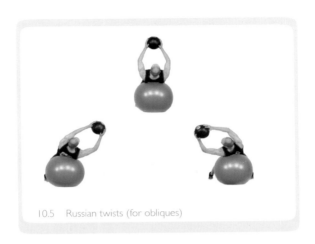

10.5   Russian twists (for obliques)

10.6   Jack knife

10.7   Reverse curls (holding wallbar) – not pictured.

10.8   Lateral curls

Medicine balls

A piece of equipment so venerated by sadistic PE teachers that children grew to fear and despise them. Footballers who wore shorts to their knees and boots higher than the ankle used them to develop awesome "throw-ins"—and it worked! Once they picked up even the leaden footballs of yore, they could hurl them further. With the more modern concepts of sophisticated training (what I call the "leg-warmer" phase), they became obsolete. But the medicine ball is back! No longer resembling hardened elephant dung, shiny black leather and brightly coloured rubber varieties abound. Best to go for the 3 or 5-kilogram balls, which are easily obtainable and competitively priced.

Overhead throws

Take some overhead throws and, as the old soccer players found, you will improve upper-body strength. Release as the ball passes over your head. Obviously, works better in pairs.

10.9 Overhead throws

Standing twists

Stand with the ball held in extended yet relaxed arms, out in front of you. Turn to one side as if to give the ball to somebody behind you. Come back to the centre and

10.10 Standing twists

pause briefly before making the same manoeuvre to the other side. Repeat for set number of repetitions, or until your obliques cry for mercy.

Narrow-grip push-ups

Narrow-grip push-ups with both hands on medicine ball. This works best with the "squashy" type medicine ball, but is, in my experience, fine with the leather type.

10.11 Narrow grip push ups

Russian twists

Use for Russian twists on the exercise ball: challenging but beneficial (see fig. 10.5).

Curls

Use as "ballast" for curls on the exercise ball (see fig. 10.3).

Pass-arounds

Stand up or sit on (a comfortable) floor holding medicine ball. Pass the ball around your back, return it to the front, and continue in this fashion for a set number of reps before passing it around in the other direction.

10.12 Passarounds

Front raise

Stand with ball held in front of thighs. Raise arms slowly to shoulder height and slowly back down again. I have found this develops your ability to hold your hands up for boxing. Best done over a time period, as opposed to repetitions, as the objective is to comfortably maintain the raise over longer time periods.

10.13 Front raise

Bouncing sit-ups

I dislike the term "sit-up" but it best describes the action required. Sit back in front of a brick wall (not a plastered wall!) with bent knees. As you come up release with a two-handed throw against the wall and catch the return as you sit back. You will need the "bouncy" variety for this, as the leather variety will in this exercise be as much use as a Christmas pudding.

10.14   Chopping wood

Chopping wood

Standing, feet shoulder-width apart holding ball in both hands. Swing ball from high to low in an action akin to chopping wood. After a set number of reps, switch to the other side.

Shot putts

Launch the ball from a shot-putting stance single-handed, either to a partner or to beat a mark on the ground. Builds shoulder and arm power. This can be done with set reps, concentrating on one arm at a time, or simply with alternate arms.

10.15   Shot putts

Exercises to strengthen the abs (without equipment).[1]

Curl ups

Start with fingertips resting on the side of the head, and bent knees. "Curl" torso forward until shoulder blades, not lower back, leave the floor. After a 2-second pause lower down again.

Crunch

As above but with the legs crossed and bent at the knee, lower leg horizontal to the floor before starting. A variation is to put the feet up on a bench.

Reverse crunch

Start as with the crunch but draw the knees towards the ribs.

Oblique crunch

Place feet on bench with knees bent at right angles and fingers resting by the side of the head. Lift and turn as if to place your elbow against the opposite knee. Pause for 2 seconds before returning to the start and then perform same move to the other knee.

10.16 Oblique crunch

"The plank" (also known as "the hover" and "the bridge")

Targets the transversus abdominis.

Rest solely on your elbows and toes, your body in a straight line from the back of your head

[1] Also see *calisthenics*, p. 70.

10.17 a) The plank b) the side plank

down to your heels. Hold for 30 seconds (or as long as you can!) to start, and build up to 60 seconds.

Think this is hard? Try the side plank, its tougher cousin. Lie on your side. Raise yourself up on one elbow, with the arm bent at 90 degrees, your only other contact with the floor being the side of your lower foot. Hold for a period of time as with the plank.

With equipment you can hang from or rest on, you can do variations of most of the above. If you combine these with disciplines involving the exercise ball, the medicine ball and the power wheel, you should build good abs and a strong core.

The power wheel

Some years ago, among some of the weird and wonderful weight-reducing and slimming advertisements came a contraption that resembled the wheel of a garden wheelbarrow. It was revealed in exalted tones that a quick daily workout with this simple device would not only reduce fat but give you sculpted abdominal muscles. It was a cheap plastic wheel with a metal handle on each side and you knelt down and rolled it out in front of you.

A couple of years ago I saw the "power wheel", and, as one of the few people at the gym to remember the plastic prototype, I was not initially impressed. I was told it had been recommended by world champion shoot-fighter Erik Paulson, who regularly came over from Dan Inosanto's

Academy in Los Angeles to give his well-attended seminars. Erik is not only in possession of enormous strength and impressive physique but is also a very useful boxer who spars with professional boxers as part of his demanding training regime. In short, his point of view was to be respected.

The new wheel was a much classier looking affair, much like the front wheel of a motor-scooter, with adjustable foot-straps on the handles and a sturdy rubber tread. It also came at an enhanced price, of course!

The manufacturers claimed it improved balance and stability in the core and, in addition, the shoulders, chest, back arms, glutes and hamstrings. This was a bold claim, but after some initial scepticism, I found that, according to how hard you were prepared to work, many of these claims were about right. You can make impressive core strength gains with the wheel, but there are some points you need to bear in mind before launching into it:

1   you must be warmed up thoroughly

2   you should already be at a fairly good level of fitness

3   you will need a well-padded surface for your knees, to start with. A judo mat, a firm exercise mat, or carpet is fine.

The velcro-fastening straps and pedals on the side of the wheel mean you can perform push-ups, plyo-jumps, pikes and other assorted moves— all with great difficulty! Due to the highly unstable mode of transport you are balanced on, a huge number of muscles are recruited just to keep you from crumpling to the floor: something most people do initially, until they learn to adapt.

In my experience, there is much core training which you have to hope is all working towards a result; the wheel is the one where you feel the effects almost immediately, especially if you become over-enthusiastic.

It really can be a great boon to improving your core strength, but I must stress it should be approached with caution. It will not suit everybody.

10.18   Power wheel

11. Circuit training

The beauty of circuit training is its flexibility and its adaptability to provide specific training for individual sports. It involves a frequent change of training activity, performed in rapid succession, with very little rest between exercise "stations".

A boxing circuit needs to allow the trainer to rehearse various moves and techniques, leading to improved strength and endurance. There is very little emphasis placed on skill factors.

I have been supervising a circuit class of this nature at Bob Breen's Academy for more years than I care to remember, and have found the best system for my class is one that spreads out the pushing and pulling exercises, so that they are never consecutive. This allows the smaller muscle groups (biceps and triceps) to recover. I also spread out the leg exercises, as it would be detrimental to perform deadlifts, lunges or squats too soon after one another. I always include two sessions of skipping (which is always used for the warm-up), two sessions of shuttle-running, and two sessions of bagwork, one on the light bag and one on the heavy bag.

The circuits always contain exercises that work the large muscle groups—bench-press, squats and deadlifts—as well as abdominal work of varying difficulty.

I have recently found many of the "core training" disciplines introduced to be effective—I hesitate to use the word "popular". We often include exercises involving the Swiss ball, medicine balls and the "power wheel" (see section on exercises with these concepts).

Warm-up should consist of 5-10 minutes of easy skipping or shadow boxing, followed by a short stretch. Cooldown should be relaxed skipping for 5 minutes, with a floor-based stretch of 30 seconds per body part to conclude.

There are no hard and fixed rules with circuit training, and you can quite easily construct your own circuit at home, even without equipment. You could warm up with jogging or shadow-boxing, have a short stretch, and then go through a regime of push-ups, crunches, back extensions, tricep dips, squats, lunges, step-ups (on stairs), calf raises, tuck jumps and shuttle runs.

Obviously, if you were to add home-friendly portable equipment you could become more versatile. You could incorporate the use of a Swiss ball, a medicine ball, some light weights and Tubi-grip. Tubi-grip is extremely versatile and reasonably inexpensive. It comes in a variety of strengths which are colour-coded (black being the most resistant). It allows you to do squats, curls, upright rows and, when looped around a solid support, seated rows, lat pull-downs and resistance punching exercises.

11.1   Squats using Tubi-grip

Circuits can be multi-stationed or sparsely laid out to suit individual needs. The two circuits I have shown overleaf are purely suggestions to give some idea of how to spread out a circular circuit, or how to use a linear model. The main considerations are time, space availability and equipment.

11.2   Bicep curl using Tubi-grip

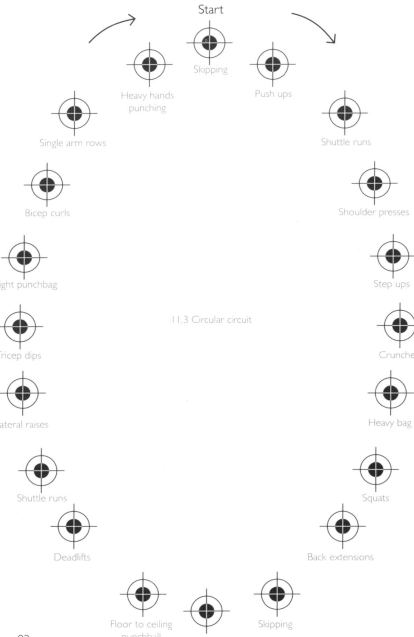

Start

Skipping

Heavy hands
punching

Push ups

Single arm rows

Shuttle runs

Bicep curls

Shoulder presses

Light punchbag

Step ups

Tricep dips

Crunches

Lateral raises

Heavy bag

Shuttle runs

Squats

Deadlifts

Back extensions

Floor to ceiling
punchball

Reverse curls

Skipping

11.3 Circular circuit

Start

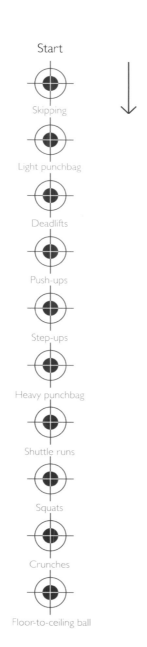

Skipping

Light punchbag

Deadlifts

Push-ups

11.4 Linear circuit

Step-ups

Heavy punchbag

Shuttle runs

Squats

Crunches

Floor-to-ceiling ball

12. Training with a partner

It is a boon to have a sympathetic training partner. Together you can work progressively to improve all aspects of technique and fitness. As you become more proficient, you will share your ideas and help each other develop. You should be capable of receiving constructive criticism from your partner, like "you are dropping your hands" or "you are sticking your chin out", and be grateful for the advice. You can work a system of "one on, one off" whereby you take turns at training drills with one working hard, one recovering briefly, but exhorting the partner to work even harder.

Do not, however, become totally dependent on your partner; have a back-up plan. There will be times, inevitably, when they will get stuck at work or in traffic, thus giving you the opportunity to duck a potentially tough session. In this case, train alone to the best of your ability (see *solo training workout*, p. 102).

Drills

Here are some of the partner drills we use, but be imaginative and try to develop your own. Change them regularly to avoid them becoming stale or boring.

Circling the pad

Put a focus pad on the floor and start out by facing each other a few feet apart. Move around the pad, shadow-boxing as you go, forcing your partner to retreat in a circular direction. Switch direction frequently and take turns at being the instigator of the movement.

12.1   Circling the pad

Crunch and punch

The striker, in bag mitts, starts by lying in a "pre-crunch" position, with the standing pad-holder treading lightly on his toes. After a predetermined number of abs crunches, the striker leaps to his feet and throws a rapid burst of punches. Start out with 10 crunches and 10 punches for 3 sets before switching roles. It's harder than it sounds and should be performed in a rapid anaerobic manner. As you get fitter, increase the repetitions and the sets.

12.2   Crunch and punch

Slap and turn

Striker faces away from the pad-holder, who then slaps him on the back. At this signal the striker spins around and responds to the angle of the proffered pads as to whether to jab, hook, cross etc. as required. This is best done to a time limit, say 1 or 2 minutes to start with, before switching roles.

12.3   Slap and turn

Hide the pads

Pad-holder moves around with pads held behind and then produces them suddenly, requiring an instant response from the striker.

12.4   Hide the pads

Hit and run

Striker punches rapidly, with pad-holder calling the shots and then instantly retreats on their completion before the holder can reply with a light (or otherwise) cuff with the focus pad.

12.5   Hit and run

12.6   Two vs. One

Two vs. One

Striker has to deal with two holders coming at him or her, giving awkward unexpected angles and approaches to deal with as the holders advance and retreat. Particularly good for sharpening reaction time and keeping composure under pressure.

Stamina drill

Continuous rapid-fire punches on focus pads for 2 minutes with a half minute break between rounds. Start with 2 rounds and build up in number as stamina improves.

Ducking the rope

A long length of rope is attached to a convenient fixture at one end at about neck height. One partner lifts and lowers rope as the other bobs and weaves from side to side, complying with the variance in height.

12.7   Ducking the rope

The holder instructs when to advance and when to retreat.

12.8   Duck and jump

Duck and jump

One partner holds a broomstick out in front and sweeps it slowly from side to side forcing the other to jump over the low sweeps and duck under the high ones. Perform slowly to begin with and speed up with proficiency.

Oblique swings

One partner swings a rope obliquely from one side to the other as if forming a large letter "v". The partner avoids the rope by "angling" in and out of the sweeps.

12.9   Oblique swings

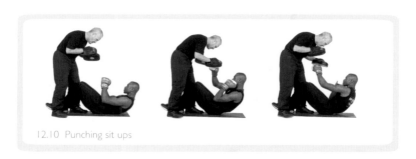

12.10 Punching sit ups

Punching sit-ups

One partner, wearing bag mitts, lies on his back with knees slightly bent. The other holds the pads over him or her to start hitting them from a prone position, and gradually withdraws the pads so the striker has to slowly rise to make good contact. Once in a full sitting position, the action is reversed, forcing him or her all the way back down again while hitting continuously. Predetermine a set number or time factor. Start easily and gradually build up intensity and output.

The underarm glove

12.11 Underarm glove

One partner wears one focus pad, held up to be suitable for a jab or hook. The striker, in bag mitts, retains another bag mitt under his bicep, pressed against his ribcage. This reinforces the correct position of the non-striking arm during the hitting action, protecting the ribs. If the striker, throwing jabs, double-jabs and hooks as instructed, allows the mitt to drop, a suitable penalty is imposed, such as press-ups or payment of post-training refreshments.

13. The solo training workout

1	Skip 2 minutes
2	Short stretch (all major muscle groups) 8-10 seconds each stretch
3	Shadow box 2 minutes
4	Heavy bag—hit light and fast 2 minutes
5	Skip 2 minutes
6	Abs crunches 30 reps
7	Push-ups 30 reps
8	Skip 1 minute—top speed (use speed rope)
9	Step-ups on reebok step-box/sturdy crate with 5-10kg weights, 20 reps
10	Shadow box 2 minutes
11	Box jumps (2 footed jumps on/off step-box to alternate sides) 1 minute
12	Squats with 5-10kg weights 20 reps

13	Skip 2 minutes
14	Hooks and uppercuts on "teardrop" or maize bag (or any available bag) 2 minutes
15	Shuttle runs (doggies) 2 minutes
16	Crunches 30 reps
17	Push-ups 30 reps
18	Skip 2 minutes
19	Heavy bag—hitting hard—2 minutes
20	Squats (as before) 20 reps
21	Shadow box 2 minutes
22	Step-ups (as before)
23	Skip 2 minutes
24	Box-jumps (as before) 1 minute
25	Shadow box 2 minutes
26	Shuttle runs 2 minutes
27	Skip (slow pace) 2 minutes
28	Long stretch—30 seconds each muscle group
29	Shake-out limbs and gentle mobility movements

Notes

For beginners—halve times

For advanced—increase times and weights, shadow box with small hand weights, use power wheel for abs and push-up exercises and use a weighted skipping rope.

Sip fluids constantly, re-stretch if feeling "tight", and take a 1 minute break at intervals if unused to this type of training.

training tip

You may find that some motivational music will help, especially to get a rhythm whilst skipping.

Equipment required

Skipping ropes—ideally heavy rope and speed rope.

Bag mitts; floor mat; step-box or sturdy crate.

5-10kg weights.

training tip

Vale Tudo instructor Matt Chapman records his workouts on audio tape for his students to take away to their home or own gym. Tape your own, adapted to your requirements.

13.1   Equipment used in the solo training workout

Solo training workout.		1	2	3
1	Skip 2 minutes			
2	Short stretch (all major muscle groups) 8-10 seconds each stretch			
3	Shadow box 2 minutes			
4	Heavy bag—hit light and fast 2 minutes			
5	Skip 2 minutes			
6	Abs crunches 30 reps			
7	Push-ups 30 reps			
8	Skip 1 minute—top speed (use speed rope)			
9	Step-ups on Reebok step-box/ sturdy crate with 5-10kg weights, 20 reps			
10	Shadow box 2 minutes			
11	Box jumps 1 minute (2 footed jumps on/off step-box to alternate sides)			
12	Squats with 5-10kg weights 20 reps			
13	Skip 2 minutes			

Photocopiable page © Ian Oliver 2005

		1	2	3
14	Hooks & uppercuts on "teardrop" or maize bag (or any available bag) 2 minutes			
15	Shuttle runs (doggies) 2 minutes			
16	Crunches 30 reps			
17	Push-ups 30 reps			
18	Skip 2 minutes			
19	Heavy bag, hitting hard—2 minutes			
20	Squats (as before)			
21	Shadow box 2 minutes			
22	Step-ups (as before)			
23	Skip 2 minutes			
24	Box-jumps (as before) 1 minute			
25	Shadow box 2 minutes			
26	Shuttle runs 2 minutes			
27	Skip (slow pace) 2 minutes			
28	Long stretch—30 seconds each muscle group			
29	Shake-out limbs and gentle mobility movements			

Photocopiable page © Ian Oliver 2005

14. Advanced training

The following training disciplines are aimed at those with a fairly good level of fitness. The weight training/power lifting section, for example, requires working with an Olympic bar, which weighs 22 kilograms unloaded. Some of the plyometric drills should not be attempted by anybody with a history of, or current, knee or back problems. These drills are a system to improve fitness for the already quite fit person; it is highly inadvisable for unfit individuals to attempt them. If in any doubt speak to a qualified fitness professional before commencing a programme involving advanced training of any nature.

Advanced Weight Training

The earlier chapter on weight training is, hopefully, adequate to provide for the strength needs of the majority of people, but in fairness to those who need serious strength gains, I have added the following disciplines, mainly derived from power lifting, a sport in its own right. Boxing requires all-round body strength: the chest and back muscles are responsible for the throwing and retraction of punches; the legs provide push-off power and stability for both offensive and defensive actions. The following may prove useful for anybody whose strength gains have reached a plateau, or those seeking to explore the potential for explosive power. These exercises may require professional tutelage, and as I have already suggested, seek the advice of a qualified instructor, which will almost certainly be the case if you have never attempted any of these disciplines before.

Before you start:

Breathing

I was taught, after what now seems to be just after the Fall of Rome, to inhale prior to the lift, and exhale on the lift. Using the bench press as an example, inhale as you lower (eccentric) — exhale as you press the bar up (concentric). I find a crude, but helpful, maxim is "blow on the effort". NEVER attempt to complete a lift while holding your breath; this will deprive your brain of oxygen, with disastrous results a possibility. A blackout while supporting a heavy bar does not bear thinking about.

Speed

Work slowly at all times in order to recruit the maximum amount of muscle fibre. There is no reason for speed in any of the following exercises.

Working slowly encourages good technique and proper control.

Safety

Always use a spotter if there is one available. A decent gym will usually be in a position to provide assistance for a short time if you do not have a training partner, which is the most advisable solution. Always use collars on both bars and dumbbells; check if Allen bolts are tight, even if prior users neglect to do so. Using a mirror serves two purposes (checking hair and biceps not, as many seem to feel, being one of them); firstly to aid checking for good alignment to ensure personal safety, and secondly to check for the approach of unaware or ignorant gym users. Clear away obstacles and ensure good clearance behind you. Squatting down only to jam your backside into a bench and hurtle forwards while supporting a barbell is a recipe for disaster (but I have seen it happen). DO NOT OVERLOAD. We were once hailed by screams from the free weights room to find a young guy trapped under 80 kilos of ironware pinning him to the bench. He had been under the (mistaken) impression he could bench press this amount. Know your limits; never feel too proud to strip down the previous user's bar. Chances are he or she is a more advanced trainer, or has different specifics.

The Exercises

Barbell Clean and Press   *(for legs, back and shoulders)*

Stand behind barbell (use an Olympic bar if possible) with feet shoulder-width apart. The very tips of the toes should be visible from above, and shins should be close to the bar. Bend knees to start lift, hands slightly wider than shoulders as you grip the bar, but keep

14.1   Barbell clean and press

head up, eyes looking upward to maintain safe back position. Lift the bar in one slow, fluid movement to shoulder height, flipping the palms of the hands over to support the bar, which should rest on the upper chest prior to the upward press. Press overhead until the arms are fully extended. Reverse the procedure to lower the bar back to the chest, and then flipping the hands forward, lower the bar to the floor, touching the plates down lightly before continuing. Start with an unloaded bar as a rehearsal; in the first sessions perform only a few repetitions, adding more as you grow accustomed to the lift.

Bench Press   *(for chest, anterior deltoids, triceps)*

Grip the bar, ideally an Olympic barbell, slightly wider than shoulder-width. Ensure back is flat and feet firmly planted on the floor. Lower the bar to the chest, inhaling as you do so. Exhale as you drive the bar upward to arm's length. Pause for a second at the top and bottom of the lift. Take about 3 seconds to lift and the same to lower; count the seconds to yourself to perfect your timing. A spotter is recommended for heavy lifts. If training alone be absolutely certainly the weight is comfortably within your capacity, to eliminate the risk of injury and embarrassment.

14.2   Bench press

Incline Barbell Bench Press   *(upper chest, anterior deltoids)*

Using a barbell the bench should be set at 45 degrees in a squat rack, or Smith machine. If neither is available the exercise can be performed with dumbbells. For bar – grip slightly wider than shoulders; for dumbbells hold out level with the shoulders, the elbows pulled back. Palms may face forwards, or facing each other if this makes it easier. Getting heavy dumbbells into place without a partner to hand them to you can be tricky. One solution is to place them onto the thighs one at a time, then lift them, also one at a time, to get into the starting position, reversing the procedure when lowering. Whether using bar or dumbbells, take 3 seconds both in lifting and lowering, with a pause at the top and bottom of the lift. Breathing is as for bench press.

14.3   Incline Barbell Bench Press.

Cross-bench Pullover   *(pectorals, serratus [ribcage])*

Lie across a bench with shoulders and upper back supported and head hanging down. Plant feet firmly, ensure stability before commencement.

14.4 Cross-bench Pullover

Hold dumbbell by supporting the top plate with both hands flat against it, holding the dumbbell handle between the thumbs. Start with arms fully extended, the dumbbell vertically in line with the neck. Lower the weight in a gentle arc to reach over and beyond the head. Return to starting position, returning in the same plane. Inhale on lowering, exhale on lifting.

Seated Leg Press   (Quads)

Where no leg press machine is available substitute squats (heavy weights, low reps). Once seated on the leg press machine ensure the legs describe a right angle, adjusting the seat to enable this. Push plate away slowly and steadily making sure your backside never leaves the seat; keep your head and back

14.5   Seated Leg Press

in upright, i.e. not craning forward. Keep all of the soles of both feet firmly in place, the feet in line with the knees. Great care should be taken with this machine to ensure maximum safety.

Squats with Barbell (quads, glutes)

As in chapter 8, but using the Olympic bar with a spotter or a Smith machine or squat rack. With the barbell option start as if performing no.1 i.e. the barbell clean and press, but at the "press" stage bring the bar over your head to rest across the middle of the shoulders and upper back, NOT the neck. Some gyms provide a padded wrap to prevent "bite" from the bar, self-help comes in the form of a folded hand-towel, the more macho element disdaining both. In reality once you get used to proper placement padding usually becomes superfluous. Grip the bar as far out to the plates as is manageable, feet shoulder-width apart or slightly wider, toes turned out slightly. As you bend the knees, attempting to get the upper leg parallel to the floor, keep eyes upward and back straight. Do not allow your heels to lift off the floor; some people have

14.6   Squats with Barbell

great difficulty in achieving this, in which case block the heels with a wooden slat 1" - 2" long, or a light, thin plate (a 2.5 kilo Olympic plate will suffice) under each heel. Reverse the procedure to return the bar to the floor.

Experienced weight trainers will often use a "superset" routine, doing two or three exercise for one particular body part in succession. For the slightly less experienced I would advocate alternating between upper and lower body, (especially if you want to walk with a modicum of normality the following day).

Rehearse all the exercises WITHOUT a weight beforehand to achieve correct technique and control. Do not be afraid of looking stupid, throwing your back out by virtue of bad technique is a great deal more stupid.

Sample workout

Sample workout

Warm up	5 -10 mins
Barbell Power Clean and Press	
Bench Press	
Squats	
Incline Bench Press	
Seated Leg Press	
Cross Bench Pullovers	
Warm down	5-10 mins

IMPORTANT

Stretch all body parts (15.1 - 15.5 page 124 onwards) for at least 30 seconds each, to prevent soreness and speed recovery from your exertions. I do not advise doing this kind of workout more than once a week unless you are extremely fit and extremely competent.

Plyometrics

A boxer's power is derived from push-off from the legs, trunk rotation and strong arm and shoulder movement. Plyometrics are explosive movements used in an effort designed to improve power (force x velocity). It is wise to start with the most basic exercises, requiring the minimum effort, to gain confidence and acquire the motor skills required, in order to avoid injury in what can be quite demanding, if uncomplicated, procedures. These exercises are not recommended for anybody with back or knee problems.

While plyometric exercises can improve power, you need to be fit before attempting them. The simplest example of a plyometric excise is hopping, so anybody who was a virtuoso at hopscotch starts with an advantage.

The Exercises

Depth Jumps

Stand on a box 1 - 2 feet high (e.g. 2 x step boxes).

Jump from box to land softly and explode upward reaching as high as possible.

Optional addition; after landing jump over a barrier, (hurdle, box etc.)

14.7   Depth jumps

Stick Jumps

Set 4 sticks on the floor (as shown). Take off sideways, pushing off with the left foot to land with the right. Attempt to land softly and firmly, holding the position for a second before returning. Do 20 reps to start with.

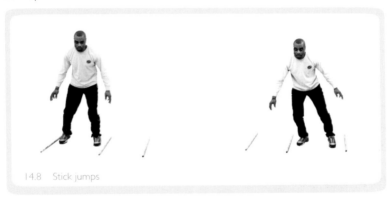

14.8 Stick jumps

Tuck Jumps

Start with feet shoulder-width apart. Half squat before making a vertical take-off, bringing the knees up towards the chest. Land softly with bent knees to absorb shock. Take a few light bounces on the spot before "taking-off" again.

14.9 Tuck jumps

Hurdles

Assemble hurdles that will be knocked aside on impact, as opposed to the kind you might trip over, as knocking yourself unconscious defeats the object of the manoeuvre. Use sticks, (garden canes, cut-down broom handles etc), resting across step-boxes or upturned plastic buckets. Nice shiny tailor-made hurdles are available, don't lash out on them until you become a competent hurdler. Jump 3 hurdles, turn and come back, completing 4 repetitions, (12 jumps in total) to begin with. Start with two footed variety, move on to one-legged jumps.

Optional addition; combine with Depth Jumps (fig. 14.7).

14.10 Hurdles

Explosive press-ups (from incline)

Start in the lowered press-up position, feet elevated on a step-box. Push off powerfully to land with your hands wider than your shoulders. Return to the start position before the next repetition. For increased difficulty push off when returning from the wide position to the original.

14.11 Explosive press-ups

Punchbag Thrust

Push a heavy punch bag away with a vigorous shoulder turn, then arrest its return with the same hand in a positive action. Start with 10 on the left, 10 on the right, then 10 with both hands. Make certain no unsuspecting gym patrons are within flattening range before launching your missile, or you may need to find another gym to perfect your "shove/ shock" routine.

I particularly like this manoeuvre as I feel it is boxing-specific. Most plyometric manuals give specific exercises for figure-skating, netball, speed-skating and just about every sport imaginable, but I have yet to see any relating to boxing.

14.12 Punchbag trust

Advanced Boxing Drills

Moving Target

Pad-holder holds as for jab, cross, hooks and uppercuts but not, as before, in a static pose. The pads are kept on the move, providing a more challenging task for the hitter. Do not

14.13 Moving target

throw full-blooded punches as a miss of this nature could prove unkind to your elbow.

Defence Drills

a) JAB; block left jab with a semi-clenched right glove, "fielding" the punch with a semi-catch technique - don't slap it away. Wait until the jab passes your own left lead before blocking, going out to meet the anticipated blow can leave a large gap, rendering you open to a hook-off-the-jab.

14.14 Defence Drills: Jab

b) STRAIGHT RIGHT; Steer incoming punch away with your left hand, or turn the shoulder, your right hand alongside it covering your chin, to nullify the impact.

14.15 Defence Drills: Straight right

c) HOOKS; a choice of 3:

   i) block with raised arm

14.16 Defence Drills: block hook with raised arm

ii) bob and weave (impractical against a much shorter opponent)

14.17 Defence Drills: bob and weave

iii) sway-back to avoid the blow.

14.18 Defence Drills: sway back

Perform these drills in sparring gloves, gradually increasing the speed and intensity. These drills can be considered a precursor to actual sparring. Start by alternating with your partner and progress to both throwing punches at random in a deliberate fashion.

Slo-Mo Sparring

Just as the title implies, throw all punches in a slow, deliberate fashion, wearing 14-18 ounce gloves and mouth guards. Agree beforehand on the "degree of intensity", particularly if you want to keep your sparring partner. Headguards are a matter of personal choice. I tend to discourage beginners from wearing them as they give a false sense of security and can lead to a cavalier attitude to head shots. Some headguards have a poor design and can hinder the vision when the head is turned.

"Backs to the Wall" Defence

Stand with back to the gym wall. Partner throws slo-mo punches at random to head and body in (hopefully) friendly fashion. Block and evade punches – without coming away from the wall or returning punches, no matter how tempting it may be! Start with one 2 minute round, progressing to 3-5 rounds. Knowing it's your partner's turn to throw punches next should encourage friendly punches. Large sparring gloves and mouth guards are essential for this drill.

14.19 Backs to the wall defence

15. Flexibility and stretching

Flexibility is an important part of training to your maximum ability. It can improve your performance as well as reduce the risk of injury. Post-exercise stretches will speed your recovery from hard training, in addition to maintaining, or further developing, your level of flexibility.

Thus, your training should usually encompass the following phases: the warm-up; the workout; the warm-down; the warm-down stretch.

The warm-up

Cold muscles do not enjoy being stretched. Think of putty or plasticine before you have warmed it in your hands before use; if you tried to do anything with it in its cold state it would simply tear. Warming-up is essential for two main reasons:

1   the body functions better when warm, enabling the muscles to become more pliable

2   the warm-up gets you "in the mood", preparing the mind for the action to follow.

Muscles at rest need only 15% of total blood flow, whereas high activity requires 80% of total blood flow as the muscles demand more fuel. The transfer of the supply cannot happen quickly, and so warm-up should be anything from 5-15 minutes according to the individual, the intended level of exertion or the coach's judgement.

The activity should be continuous, rhythmic and, ideally, specific or relative to the upcoming workout. It follows logically that a good warm-up activity for boxing will involve skipping and/or shadow boxing. Always ensure you wear enough clothing to stay warm; you can always shed your outer layers when you get warmed up.

To stretch or not to stretch? This has now become the question. For years we were told to warm-up, mobilise joints, and to have a short pre-exercise stretch. This would take less than a minute in total, stretching for 6-8 seconds per body part. The stretch was always performed standing, as it was considered that lying down or sitting would allow the body to cool, to the obvious detriment of the warm-up.

Suddenly—all change! Fitness gurus seem unable to come to a unified agreement on the subject of stretching before the workout. Recent data suggests that stretching works by subjecting muscles to stress, and the stress applied to muscles and joints tends to leave them unready for, and even vulnerable to, vigorous exercise. If you, like me, have been doing a short stretch for years with no noticeable ill-effects, my advice would be to carry on regardless.

Experiment: try skipping your stretch and see if it makes any discernible difference.

In either case, I am sure there is nothing pernicious about a 6-second gentle stretch before a 5-mile run. The sports physiology community changes its opinion of what is best at such a dazzling pace, I half expect it to change again in a short time.

One point all fitness instructors will agree upon is that the optimal time for stretching is after your workout, when the muscles are blood-enriched, warm and, therefore, pliable. It will help to speed your recovery, reduce muscular soreness and begin the process of waste clearance.

The warm-down

After your workout it is essential to warm down. Sudden cessation of exercise can be harmful to the heart. It also helps to clear lactic acid and reduces muscle soreness; anyone who has suffered the dreaded D.O.M.S (delayed onset muscle soreness) will appreciate the wisdom of avoiding this particular agony by a warm-down and stretch. If, like me, you spent the three days after running a marathon coming downstairs backwards, you will know just what I mean; sadly, the last thing anyone wants to do after completing a marathon is any further form of exertion! Your warm-down should be similar in content and duration to your warm-up.

Ballistic stretching

Involves bouncing movements and is highly inadvisable, as the movement lacks the required control and does not allow the muscles to stretch adequately. Taken to the extreme it can cause soreness and injury. Best left to finely tuned, specialised athletes, supervised by experienced coaches. Stretch slowly: don't bounce!

The warm-down stretch

You can avail yourself of any number of books on flexibility which vary in how much technical information they contain. I have worked on the basis that for now what you need to know is:

1   which muscles to stretch

2   how to do them.

I prefer to start at the top and work down, in the hope I won't overlook any parts in the descent; many prefer to work their way up instead. All stretches listed from page 124 onwards require no walls, boxes or other equipment.

Finish of by mobilising neck, shoulders, hips and ankles. Shake out arms and legs and take a warm shower.

Developmental stretching

The system I find useful, and have found successful with my students, is a simple contract-relax technique. It can be done with a partner or, in the case of some muscle groups, by yourself. The example used is for developing flexibility in the hamstrings.

Stand in front of a surface of about waist height; a weights rack or a stack of step boxes is ideal. With the toe of the standing foot facing forward, raise the other leg to rest on the raised surface or box. Reach as far as possible towards the toe of the raised foot. Stop when you have reached as far as you can: when you feel uncomfortable, and get the sensation often referred to as "the bite". Now you will need a little courage, as you hold that uncomfortable position for about 10-20 seconds. To your surprise and relief, this tight and slightly painful feeling wears off.

Exhale and reach forward another inch or so, and start the process all over again. Inch-by-inch and week-by-week you are educating your muscles to develop more flexibility by tolerating these minute advances. Needless to say it will take some sticking power on your part, but if you want to improve flexibility it definitely works; you can use the same technique to improve your range in doing "the splits". If the same stretch is performed with a partner, they can hold your foot, raising it carefully and slowly to the point of maximum contraction.

There are other techniques varying in procedure, and countless books dedicated to the subject that will explain how this works, and inform you of Golgi tendons, autogenic inhibition and all the internal mysteries of stretching. Two I have personally found informative are:

The Complete Guide to Stretching—Christopher M. Norris

Sport Stretch—Michael J Alter.

The first book is new and bang up to date. Alter's book is a few years old but has proved very popular with my students. Both books are in my public library; check them out in your own library. You may even find other books that can help you more.

If you feel you are inflexible, do not settle for it by consoling yourself with such excuses as:

> *"It's my age"*–you can improve your flexibility, or at least protect what you have if you stretch regularly
>
> *"I've never been flexible"*–there's no time like the present to improve. Get into a habit of stretching on a daily basis.

Don't sneer at disciplines like yoga or Pilates; they are no longer considered the preserve of tree-huggers or the brown rice and sandal brigade. Many elite martial artists have incorporated both as an essential aid to their training regime. People of all ages have benefited enormously from yoga, in particular.

Flexibility is the best example of a hackneyed, but true, maxim: use it or lose it.

The stretches

15.1   Shoulder stretch

15.2   Spinal muscles—"angry cat"

15.3   Back, standing

15.4   Chest

15.5   Lower back

15.6   Obliques

15.7   Glutes

15.8   Hamstrings

15.9   Quads

15.10 Hip flexors

15.11 Adductors

15.12 Calf

15.13 Soleus and Achilles

15.14 Triceps

15.15 Neck

16. Alternative training

Running is a specific training tool for boxing, and has been a traditional endurance system for countless years. But if the weather is foul (deep snow, stormy or foggy) and unless there is a treadmill available, running is out. Also, if you are suffering from a strained calf muscle or Achilles tendon, you would be unwise to run. You still want to maintain your aerobic fitness, so you may need to train in a way that reduces impact or overuse, in the short term, until you can resume running. If you have to seek an alternative training form, look for something that will provide interest or variety. Combining various systems, the popularity of which is mainly due to the growth of triathlon training, is often referred to as cross-training. Training should be specific for your sport, but if no other forms of aerobic training are possible, try static or road cycling, Concept rower (or similar static rower), Stairmaster and swimming. Look to achieve a 30-45 minute session.

Here is a suggested workout. (I have limited the cycling section to

1	Static cycle (on Schwinn "Airdyne" or similar) 10 minutes @ 40-60 revs per minute.
2	Row (on "Concept" rower or similar: 15 minutes @ 28-40 strokes per minute on setting 5).
3	Stairmaster; use "intervals" setting, level 5-8 or manual setting of choice. (Always leave to last. Starting on the Stairmaster when cold can be harsh on the calf muscles.)

10 minutes as I have known people start to lose the will to live if it goes any longer.)

Stretch beforehand (6-8 seconds muscle group) and (30 seconds per muscle group).

Swimming

The all-round muscle toner, superb if you are recovering from injury. Swimming places less stress than other cross-training activities on muscles, bones and joints, whilst improving muscular and cardiovascular strength and flexibility. In his biography *The Tartan Terror* (a great read), Kenny Buchanan, the legendary former world lightweight champion, attributed his terrific lung power to the huge number of lengths he swam underwater at his local baths. Warm up at first with a few easy lengths, especially if you have not swum lately. Consider interval training, alternating speed and recovery lengths.

Aerobic classes

So many guys will not touch an aerobics class with a ten-foot bargepole, as they consider it to be too "girly". Due to the influx of jazzercise, boxercise, Tae Bo and numerous new exercise classes, aerobics has taken a bit of a back seat. Ironically, it is a good accompaniment to boxing, as most classes contain elements that call for balance and co-ordination. It will also improve cardiovascular capacity and muscular endurance. I have known guys dragged along kicking and screaming by their girlfriends or wives to classes, but have never known any of them to admit they were not exhausted by the end. Like most exercise classes of this nature, the quality of training hinges on the ability of the instructor.

17. Equipment

For your specific boxing training needs, there are some obvious requirements you will need straight away, and there are other items you can add as you progress.

Bag mitts

Essential requirement. Always go for good quality leather ones; the vinyl type tend to wear quickly, offer less protection and split easily. I think from this you may have observed that I am no fan of them. Make sure you have a little room in your new gloves, there being two reasons for this:

your hands will become hot if you wear the gloves for a long session, and they will expand. Snug-fitting gloves will prove uncomfortable.

you will possibly want to wrap your hands, especially if you work on the heavy bag. Leave enough room for the wraps.

Good quality gloves come in small, medium and large, so you should find a good fit. At our gym, and, I imagine, a great many others, is a row of boxes filled with long-abandoned gloves in which people can, in the interests of economy, take a "lucky dip". I feel this is a false

17.1 Thumbless bag mitts

economy, unless you enjoy your hands reeking with the strong odour of performing seals that no soap known to mankind can neutralise for days.

Avoid this phenomenon occurring with your own gloves by giving them a regular shot of Dettox, which kills off bacteria. Return to your schooldays, and write your name on them for that occasion when you stumble dazed and confused from the gym leaving them behind. Phoning to report them missing to the gym will not be helped by the information that "they are red".

Focus pads (hook and jab pads)

Again go for the best leather variety you can afford. The vinyl ones fall far short of what is required, and the canvas ones soon take on the consistency of bread pudding: hardly conducive to "feedback".

Handwraps

Get the elasticated variety, which are less likely to become unravelled with use. These have a velcro fastening; the ones that need tying require outside help. Your wraps will lessen any abrasive rubbing from the glove, and assist in keeping a straight wrist: in line with the knuckles and not "cocked", which causes wrist injury (see section on *handwraps,* p. 145).

Sparring equipment

Sparring gloves

These tend to vary with the size of the user. They are not just to protect your sparring partner's head, but also the relatively fragile bones of the hand. Small women will require 14 oz. gloves, but most guys need 16 oz., or even 18 oz. "pillows". The reputable brands make them in all weights; buy the best you can afford. Treat them properly and they will last for years. Never put them down on the floor, they can pick up bacteria, which, above all, shows a marked lack of respect for your partner. Write your name on them and "dettox" them regularly, as this will prevent them from forming penicillin between sessions.

Mouthguard / gumshield

Mandatory for sparring. You have, to my knowledge, only two choices here; one is cheap and the other is expensive. There is a type that comes already moulded: do not even consider these.

> The do-it yourself. These were initially poor quality, but the newer variety is extremely good. You simply drop it in hot water to make it malleable, pop into your mouth, bite down and hold for 10 seconds, then immerse in cold water to set. At the time of writing these cost only £2-£3.

> Reach for your credit card as this next version involves your dentist, who will, at a price, make a perfect tailor-made mouthguard by taking an impression in hot wax, the same method as used for false teeth.

Groin guard

Highly advisable for training. Low-priced material versions and expensive but highly effective leather versions (in boxing, generally referred to as a "cup") are available. There are readily available women's versions these days; it's not just guys who can get hurt from that errant low shot.

17.3 Groin guard

Footwear

17.4 Boxing boots

This is purely down to personal choice. Boxing boots give good grip and help with the sliding aspect of footwork. These come in "high leg" or "low leg". They are available in leather, synthetic material or a combination of both. All are fine, in my estimation. Many people are just as happy and just as competent in cross-trainers or running shoes.

Headguards

Now compulsory in amateur boxing, and the best bet if you are going in for serious sparring. The trouble with headguards is that a boxer unused to sparring without one can be a trifle cavalier about taking head shots, treating the headguard as insurance. Sparring without one teaches you to move the head defensively, as you should. If you are going to get one, then a good quality leather model is the only realistic option; vinyl, foam-filled headguards offer less protection and have a nasty habit of slipping about, thus needing constant adjustment. A decent brand-name headguard, which are sized for a good fit, will not shift about

17.5 Headguard, mouthguard, 16oz sparring gloves

in combat. The version that also protects the cheekbones tends to be dearer, but offers a higher level of protection.

Handy, but non-essential kit

A countdown timer. You have a range of options:

a modestly priced countdown affair (Argos sell them)

one of those wind-up egg timers that 'ding' at zero

a stopwatch with an audible alarm

the stopwatch on your mobile phone

a sports watch, such as Casio *G shock* or Timex *Ironman* with an audible alarm

for home training, a large (you don't want to squint) cheap clock with a second hand (mine set me back £2.50 at Ikea).

Remember, if you are skipping or working on the punchbag, you do not want to interrupt your session to look at your watch; your timing device needs to be visible or audible to allow continuous training.

17.6 Timers

Dettox

Before I promote the virtues of this product, I must confirm that I have no shares in, or particular affection for, Reckitt & Coleman, the manufacturers of Dettox. A former colleague, Anthony Johnson, considered the best training tip I ever passed on to him was to treat your trainers to a light squirt of Dettox on a regular basis, thereby eliminating suspicion that they had been misused by a cat. The same goes for your gloves; worn long-term without an anti-bacterial spray, they can occasionally double as an anaesthetic.

Clean the surface of gloves and pads as well; it is inevitable that they will have spent some time on the gym floor, as well as receiving a light dressing of perspiration from time to time.

In your training bag

First of all, get the biggest, sturdiest bag you can carry, so you are always well prepared with all your kit on board.

Don't forget the:

flip-flops: avoid verrucas at all costs. They are harder to get rid of than a tattoo.

plastic bag (carrier bag will do): Keep wet stuff away from kit you need to keep dry, and avoid giving your bag that "swimming bath" odour.

water bottle: stay hydrated, get a large one, fill from the tap and sip as you train.

lightweight speed rope: get an inexpensive plastic rope to carry, in case the ones at the gym are all in use.

log book: keep a note of your early progress if you are starting on a training program. You can write out your intended workout in advance to be fully organised when you get to the gym, or photocopy the worksheets on pages 68 and 102. You only need a small exercise book. Corey, who features in many of the photos in *Boxing Fitness*, writes down everything new he has gleaned in an A4 book, as a memo for practice drills; it is his way of committing it to memory, which I think is sound.

waterproofs: a cheap fold-up waterproof top and trousers are a good addition if your training involves outdoor work. You usually get the quality you pay for with this sort of garment.

warm-up gear: if the weather looks dubious or the gym has poor, or no heating, throw in a hooded top and a woolly hat.

Vaseline: Vaseline over the eyebrow prevents sweat from running into your eyes, making them sting and impairing your vision. It also helps protect against chafing and friction from clothing, especially new kit: anyone who has suffered the dreaded "nipple rash" will know what I mean.

boxing tape/surgical tape: to cover laces on lace-up gloves and handy for running repairs to kit.

In the washbag

Apart from shower gel and toiletries, include:

Vaseline (as explained above)

small packet of plasters

small (nail) scissors

Arnica cream (for bruises: I still believe it works)

small plastic bottle of massage oil (99% grape-seed oil, 1% lavender essence). Buy grape-seed oil in supermarkets, about £1 for a ½ litre. Essence from Body Shop, about £2

packet of clean tissues and medi-wipes.

Wrapping your hands

Wrapping your hands is a precaution I cannot recommend too highly. Many of the bones of the hand are small and extremely vulnerable to injury. Whether you are hitting the pads, the bag, or sparring, it is wise to wrap your hands. This is especially true of sparring; the skull is a great deal harder than the hand! A common injury, particularly regarding newcomers, is to the wrist. Less experienced people have a tendency to cock their wrist in what I have, fairly accurately, heard described as a "swan neck" action, which is highly likely to prove injurious to the wrist. It is for this reason that

I recommend taking the wrap a little way up the arm so that the wrist is in the middle of the protected area, thus affording the maximum amount of support. In time, novices learn to straighten the arm on impact, but even experienced boxers can still damage the wrist; if you are frequently troubled with niggling wrist injuries, consider continuing your wrapping further up the arm.

There are various ways of wrapping. The example I have given is one commonly used at our gym, but there are many variations and you may, in time, develop a system of wrapping that you think suits you best. A lot will depend on the length of the wraps; you want to protect your hand but still get your glove on without using a shoehorn. I find the slightly elasticated variety of wrap works best; they give just the right amount of pressure and are less likely to come unravelled. The price difference is minimal; at the time of going to press the elasticated version are priced at £5; a small price to pay for the protection they give. Remember, hand injuries are common and can sideline you from full training for a frustratingly long period.

Cautionary note: wash your wraps frequently. Your hands sweat profusely when wrapped and wearing gloves. Repeated use without washing can give the impression that they could crawl away on their own!

Not included above, but extremely useful, is a small bottle of Olbas Oil. If you need to clear your head, it is also useful for a "wake up" (smelling salts having been frowned upon by First Aid bodies). It also doubles as a massage oil, but keep clear of sensitive regions! Tiger Balm, Ralgex and other "hot rubs" are something that you either love or hate (I'm in the latter category), but at least everybody within a 50 yard radius will know where to locate you.

Most of the equipment used in this book is available from www. fightgear.co.uk or the telesales line on 0207 729 5789.

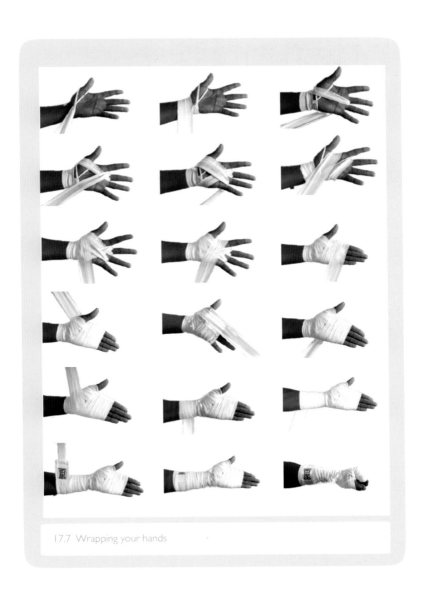

17.7 Wrapping your hands

18. Nutrition

The fuelling process—dietary advice

Anybody involved in competitive boxing will have to eat within the constraints of a diet that will not jeopardise their weight, to stay within their weight division, as well as being in top fighting shape.

As you are unlikely, at this stage, to be too concerned about making a particular weight, you can just concentrate on eating to train to the best of your capabilities. Only when you get into top shape can you consider the idea of competition. The food you eat is of the utmost importance. If you were going on a long road journey, you would automatically ensure that your fuel tank was full, and before returning you would refuel the car. So many people will put premium fuel in their car but treat their body to substandard, and often insufficient, fuel.

There are now so many worthy, informative books on sports nutrition, written by professional nutritionists, that everybody can find out exactly what they need to be eating for their specific sport. Sadly, few of them give any advice on what you require for boxing, and tend to advise on diets for running, cycling and swimming; even the good American books do the same but throw in "soccer" as well, as American women have taken to it with great success.

I have therefore put together what I hope will explain what you should be eating to get in fighting condition, using the advice I have given to students over many years. To my knowledge, none of them have died from it, and most have become very fit, or at least fitter.

Do not suddenly become monkish about it, giving up all your current diet to switch to rice and lentils. Make some gradual, tolerable changes over your training period to a more suitable source of fuel. You will very possibly find that what I advocate will not require a great deal of change from your current eating habits: just remember that if you up the level of your training, you will need an increased food supply of the right sort.

Our main source of energy comes from carbohydrate, protein and fats. Other food constituents are vitamins, minerals and water. Vitamins and minerals play essential roles in our chemical process; we all need water for all our major functions (about 60% of our body is composed of water).

Carbohydrates (hitherto referred to as carbs, for short)

These should provide the bulk of your energy, and therefore, your diet. Hard training people should aim for about 60% of their intake to be carbs. They come in two forms, simple and complex, and this can be confusing. Both simple and complex forms have nutritional value, but enter the bloodstream at different rates to be converted to glycogen for energy. This rate is listed in the glycaemic index, a system created originally to help diabetes sufferers with their insulin supply, and referred to as the GI of a foodstuff. This is not always obvious, but cornflakes have a GI of 84 (out of 100), whereas an apple registers only 38. A useful little book is *The New Glucose Revolution*, a tiny pocket book that gives a full list of the GIs of most carbs (see *helpful literature*, p. 160). This is handy when you need to know which carbs to eat before (low index) and after training (high index). This is because you will want something that will slowly release energy over your workout, and something to elevate your glucose level as soon as possible after your workout.

Unfortunately, in the Western diet we include a large amount of simple carbs from refined, concentrated sugars in such foods as biscuits, cakes, sugary breakfast cereals, buns and many similar products, and not so much of the more starch-rich carbs from plants and grains. Again, don't become too strict with yourself; just eat them in moderation. Remember not to coat the healthy options such as pasta, baked potatoes and rice in fats, such as butter or a high-fat sauce.

When advising what to eat I do, of course, accept that the individual's food tolerance and allergies will be critical to their nutrition. I will tell you that a great breakfast to start the day is a bowl of cereal with low-fat milk and a banana, but this is not of much use if you have lactic or gluten intolerance, or hate bananas. Therefore, I have just mentioned what groups to choose from, and why I feel you will need them. What you select from them must suit your individual needs.

Fruit and vegetables

Ideally you require 5 portions of fruit or vegetables a day, just for your normal dietary requirement, but more if you are training hard. When it comes to fruit and vegetables, go for as much variety as you can. When eating out, go for the fruit salad and forgo the gateau; pile on the vegetables or salad and give the fries a wide berth. All fruits have great natural nutritional benefits, but go easy on avocados, as they are high in monounsaturated fats.

Fruit juices are a convenient way of getting carbs on board, or refuelling, but read the label. Don't touch the varieties with added sugar or sweeteners; opt for natural fruit juice only.

Cereals

Breakfast cereals make not just a great start to the day. They will be fine if you get in too late to cook something but need a quick meal. Shredded Wheat and Cheerios are examples of wholegrain cereals and there are many others; read the ingredients on the side of the box before you buy. Whether you go for cereal or muesli, opt for varieties low in sugar and sodium, but high in vitamins, as found in the "fortified" varieties.

Oatmeal

Oats have nutritional value as carbs, protein, fibre and vitamins. Porridge is low in fat and has a low GI, making it a perfect breakfast food whether you prefer it with milk or water, the latter of which I would personally consider the choice of the dedicated only.

Bread

Go for the whole-grain variety, which tends to have more nutritional value than its more refined white cousin. Look also for wholegrain/wholemeal versions of pitta, tortillas and bagels to combine with a healthy protein filling (see *protein*, p. 150).

Crackers, crumpets and muffins

As with bread, go for the darker whole-grain variety. With muffins try the oatmeal or bran types as opposed to those made with white bread. Try them with jam and a negligible amount of butter if required from force of habit: don't deny yourself everything!

Pasta

High in starch yet low in fat, pasta has become the sportsperson's food of choice. The "pasta party" has been a pre-marathon ritual for years. The secret of getting the most from pasta is to not slaver high fat sauce all over it.

Go for tomato-based sauces with onions, olives, herbs, mushrooms, peppers and other vegetables, as opposed to sauces rich in cream or cheese. Try wholemeal pasta, which has more dietary fibre than its paler cousin, although the plain variety is still rich in fibre and starch.

Rice

The staple food of half the world (the slimmer half in my experience), it has numerous health benefits. It is a valuable source of starch, especially brown rice. Like pasta, it is easy to prepare, is inexpensive and needs only a simple accompaniment to provide a tasty, filling meal.

Protein

Protein plays an essential role in your diet and should ideally constitute 15-20% of your food intake. The amino acids contained in the molecular structure of muscles are built from protein. Armed with this information, many weight-trainers embark on a diet that is very high in protein. It is scientifically recorded that it is exercise, fuelled by the correct balance of carbs and protein, which builds muscle. Excessive dosage of protein in the form of expensive shakes, tuna, chicken, egg-white and other protein-rich foods that are not burnt for energy, will be stored as fat. Protein-heavy diets, to the exclusion of carbohydrate, will mean not having adequate muscle fuel required for muscular strength, development and growth. Of paramount importance is not the amount of protein you eat, but the quality.

Choice of protein

The deli is usually a good place to pick up the lean cuts of meat you need for protein. For sandwiches (for me, still the best portable refuelling method), go for chicken, turkey, beef and ham, and trim off any visible fat. Poultry has less saturated fat than red meat, if you are feeling particularly health conscious. Eat on thick wholemeal bread with low-fat spread, or mayo, mustard or ketchup instead of butter or margarine. Vary your sandwiches; sardines, tuna, salmon, boiled egg, peanut butter and, occasionally, cheese will all provide good protein. If you are training hard (women especially), you can derive your protein from milk and other dairy products. These are rich in calcium, which improves bone density, and protects against the onset of osteoporosis. Semi-skimmed or skimmed milk and low fat yoghurt are all vitamin and mineral rich. Aim to drink a half-pint minimum to a pint maximum (huge guys will get through more, I have found).

Bio-yoghurts can protect against harmful bacteria. Natural yoghurt is tasteless but combines well with fruit. Try frozen yoghurt as a substitute for ice-cream, but beware of high sugar varieties.

Beans and lentils are a good source of protein, and they reduce the risk of heart disease and maintain blood sugar levels. They have a hybrid quality, in that they provide carbohydrate as well as protein. Canned beans lose some of their vitamins but retain minerals.

Vegetarian protein

If, within your diet, there is no protein derived from meat, then it will have to come from plants. This will mean a dependence on beans, nuts, and tofu (which is made from soya beans). Protein can also be found in peanut butter and hummus (made from chickpeas). Any soya product (tofu, soy milk) is rich in protein, and vegetarians can get calcium from hard cheese, yoghurt, milk, almonds and green leafy vegetables.

Combining carbohydrates and proteins: suggested combinations

Spaghetti bolognese

Chilli con carne

Prawn risotto

Chicken curry and boiled rice

Jacket potato with baked beans or tuna

Noodles and stir-fry tofu

Greek salad with red, green and yellow peppers

Salmon and pasta salad

Salad niçoise

Chicken casserole

Shepherd's pie with vegetables

Fats

The recommendation is to have no more than 25% of your dietary intake from fat. Unfortunately most people in the West get closer to 40%. It is not just the isolated fat we eat that gets stored. Excessive carbohydrate and protein can also be converted to be stored as fat reserves if they are unused by exercise. Exercise, harnessed to a balanced diet, is the key to fat reduction. Fat contains more calories than carbohydrate or protein, and therefore eating food that is high in fat is just not conducive to good health. Just because you are fit and in a physically demanding exercise regime, it does not mean you can be cavalier about eating junk or fast food: it will prove detrimental to your training. Read the labels on cans and packaging, and whilst it is far from a foolproof solution, it will help you identify the fat content of comparable foodstuffs. All foods should give a fat content per 100 grams. Aim for 5 grams per 100 gram, and try not to go over 10 grams. The exception is oily fish, such as sardines, tuna and salmon, with their omega-3 fatty acids (the special fat found in oily fish that has numerous health benefits for the heart). When cooking, go for olive oil, which is rich in monounsaturated fat, and the healthiest choice.

Water

You need 8 glasses a day, about one and a half to two litres. Sip water as you train. It flushes away metabolic by-products. Failure to get enough water can lead to your system deriving fluid from your waste; it needs water as a coolant to regulate your temperature and this can lead to constipation. Lack of water in sporting activity can cause confusion, inability to concentrate and irrational behaviour. Tap water is fine; if you don't trust your local water, boil it first and let it cool off in the refrigerator.

The best test of whether you are drinking enough is to check the colour of your urine. If it is the colour of gin, that's excellent, if it's the colour of lager, it is a warning sign, but if it is the colour of best bitter, get some water, and quickly!

Don't overdo the water intake! Excessive amounts can have an adverse effect, leading to a sodium imbalance caused by plain water dilution.

Vitamins and minerals

If you eat a good, healthy, well-balanced diet, you do not need any vitamin or mineral supplement tablets. You should find it all in your food. While you need an adequate amount of both vitamins and minerals to function, scientific evidence, thoroughly investigative as it has been, has yet to find that additional amounts are of any benefit. Taking supplements will not harm your health but they will not prove a substitute for a poor diet. Pills cannot provide the qualities derived from fruit, vegetables and whole grains. The only possible exceptions are strict vegans, who feel they are not getting enough vitamins or minerals from a limited diet, or those recommended by a qualified physician.

Creatine

Creatine, a high energy molecule stored naturally in our muscles, teams up with phosphate to give short bursts of energy. Lately, Creatine supplements have been commonly used by both professional and recreational sportspeople. It was felt it helped in intensive bouts of exercise, and recovery from them. It has not worked for everybody: most exercisers I have discussed it with relate that it showed dynamic results initially, but the effect tapered off until it had no marked effect at all. Some, however, have continued to use Creatine in an on-and-off fashion. Low dosage and short term use would appear advisable, as the effects of using it long term are still unknown. Some people have found problems with weight gain and water retention, but in general, any side effects have been few and mild.

Sports drinks and bars

Sports bars make terrific claims about the energy they can provide, which they hope will justify the inflated price of so many of them. It is a case of reading the label; avoid those that are high in fat. A more economical alternative is the cereal bar, which should do the job of replacing energy just about as effectively, especially if teamed with a banana.

Sports drinks contain carbohydrates and so refuel more effectively than water. Some people find them unpalatable, particularly the isotonic variety. If you cannot get along with Lucozade (which, it must be said, comes in a reasonable array of flavours), Gatorade (not always easy to find in the UK), or the odd-tasting Isostar, then make your own and keep it in the fridge (see box, *DIY sportsdrink*).

DIY sportsdrink

Boil a half-litre of water, allow to cool. Add a half-litre of your favourite pure fruit juice like orange, pineapple or grapefruit. Add a pinch of salt. Mix well and refrigerate.

Smoothies are nutritious drinks, using milk or water combined with carbohydrates, for energy on the move or to refuel quickly. They are usually very high in flavour and carbs, but also in price. Get them from the supermarket and shop around. Alternatively, make your own by using a blender or food processor. My personal favourite is the banana and honey shake (see box, *Banana and honey shake*).

Banana and honey shake

You will need; one ripe banana, one pint of semi-skimmed milk, one low-fat banana flavour yoghurt, one scoop of low-fat ice-cream, a handful of ice cubes, a large spoonful of honey. Blend banana with small amount of milk. Add ice cubes and blend them in. Add the rest of the ingredients and blend on high setting. Makes 2-3 good sized servings.

Timing

Timing your food is essential. You need to eat 2-3 hours before you work out, incorporating complex carbs. You need to elevate your glucose level, as soon as possible after training, with carbohydrates, but not with a heavy meal immediately, as blood is still needed in the muscles to aid recovery.

Always eat breakfast. Keep a variety of cereals so you don't get bored with a daily bowl of cornflakes. If the only early morning place open is McDonald's, then go for a couple of English muffins with jam, orange juice and an unsweetened cup of tea. If you have arrived home late, eat something light so as not to disturb your sleep, but don't go to bed hungry. A light salad or some pasta with tomato ragu will be fine.

Carry small packs of raisins or nuts in your sports bag for those occasions when you are "starving".

Conclusion

Don't become your own food police. Eat as well and as sensibly as you can; we all have enough information these days to know the good from the bad as far as food is concerned. Never forget your overall health is far more important than your specific training needs, and any diet you choose should be one you can live well and happily on for the rest of your days. Do not be misled by the false prophets of "fad" diets that will keep you thin: they will not keep you happy. Any diet that seeks to deprive you of an adequate amount of fruit, vegetables and whole grains is not one you will need to train well.

19. Injury & illness

Combat and high impact sports can get you in great shape, but you also run the almost inevitable risk of injury, mild or otherwise.

As soon as you feel pain, stop training. If you don't know what is causing your pain, describe the symptoms to somebody who you think will know. If your injury is long-term it does not necessarily mean you cannot train at all. Do what you can within the bounds of sound sense and comfort. Leg injuries, according to severity, do not mean you can't still train your upper body, just as a sprained wrist or elbow ligament problems will not prevent leg training.

Do not put off getting a chronic problem professionally examined. If you get no satisfaction with the National Health Service (some do, some don't, in my experience), see a private specialist, preferably on recommendation. By doing so you should:

speed up the treatment

find out the root cause of your problem and how to prevent re-occurrence

find out how to "self-help" in future.

First-aid

Familiarise yourself with the basic procedure to follow if you or a training partner incurs an injury. The very minimum knowledge you should be familiar with is "RICE".

"R" is for "rest". Stop training—now!

"I" is for "ice". Get some ice, very cold water or freeze-spray applied to the area as soon as possible, and try to keep it on for 20 minutes every hour. With ice, wrap in a towel first, to prevent ice burn.

"C" is for "compression". Strap it up to prevent painful movement and limit swelling.

"E" is for "elevation". Raise injured limb to allow blood to flow back to the heart.

This is the most basic explanation of "RICE", but this little knowledge is better than nothing; obviously, if the injured person is in agony or has suffered a major trauma, do not mess about doing anything except phoning for an ambulance and making them comfortable while you wait.

A one-day first-aid course is relatively inexpensive and many local councils have them running continuously. Attending such a course counts not only for your own welfare in a crisis, but for friends, family and, more usually, total strangers. I signed up for it the day after a young guy from an opposing football team collapsed with a heart attack, and out of the many people at the ground only the referee knew what to do.

Train sensibly

Don't take unnecessary risks like carrying on when in agony, going out running on icy pavements or foggy evenings (see *alternative training,* p.134).

Try to always get a decent sleep, and don't overdo it the next day if you didn't get much sleep the night before.

Teach yourself to relax. There are numerous books in the library teaching relaxation techniques. Meditation works for many people; don't knock it until you've tried it. Chuck Norris swears by it, which got my attention.

Strains and other pains which linger on

If your muscle pull doesn't go away on its own, or returns as soon as you resume training, you may need to seek specialist advice. Sad to say, in most areas if you want speedy treatment, you are going to have to pay for it, be it an osteopath, chiropractor, physiotherapist, or sports injury specialist. It all comes down to priorities; some people will not baulk at paying £40 for a car part, but will not fork out a similar amount for a consultation about a chronic injury. Many niggling injuries can be helped with a regular massage session and, although professional treatment can prove costly, books, such as those by Mel Cash and Vivian Grisogono, that inform you how to treat your own injuries with self massage, are worth considering, especially as there is usually a wide selection at the public library.

Illness

There will, inevitably, be times when you will fall prey to the odd cold. The general rule of thumb regarding training is:

if it's from the neck up (sniffles etc.), train lightly

if it's from the neck down (aching limbs, coughing, wheezing, feeling of lethargy), do not train at all. Wait for the "all clear" before recommencement.

When returning to training after illness or injury, ease your way back into your fitness regime; you cannot catch up on lost time by overworking.

If friends or training partners tell you that you look unwell or off-colour, take notice and proceed carefully. You might be coming down with something. Curiously enough, nobody wants to share your illness, and gyms are a great place to catch something contagious or infectious, so be considerate.

Insurance

You might want to consider taking out insurance. Some gyms have it as a requirement, and it's usually as much to cover an unfortunate victim of yours as yourself personally.

The Age factor—Training for Seniors

How old is too old? I hear people of forty tell me that they are too old for this kind of training, but when they try it they are often the more committed and satisfied with their improved fitness levels. Not that many years ago, fitness classes for the over 50s consisted of gentle exercises, much of it performed while seated; a far cry from the friends I know who still do martial arts, swim for miles daily, run (not jog!) 2-3 times a week and weight-train regularly. All of them maintain flexibility by stretching regularly.

If you are reasonably fit, with no debilitating injuries and full medical clearance, and are prepared to take a patient, sensible view about your fitness aspirations, there is a great deal of boxing fitness you can participate in and derive benefit from.

A once-a-week session of light skipping, punching bags and pads, and especially weight training, jogging or running should not over-extend elderly people. Consider the vast number of 60 and 70 year olds who canter through the London Marathon (even more in the New York and Boston marathons). Flexibility training is a must for the older trainer; the term "use it or lose it" is apt in this respect. Countless tests conducted by universities in the US show that both men and women can make impressive strength gains by resistance training even into their 80s and 90s. Moderation is the key; work comfortably within your limits at first. Unfortunately injury comes all too easily to the older person and takes what seems forever to clear up. Don't write yourself off; after all, this kind of training should give you renewed confidence and self-esteem. Don't worry about what other people think. You will probably gain the grudging admiration of many younger trainers, who are hoping that they will be as fit as you when they get to your age! Take the long view and be content to build up slowly in small increments; you are unlikely to be bored.

Helpful literature DISCARD

The Lonsdale Boxing Manual David James (Robson Books)

Sports Nutrition Guidebook Nancy Clarke (Human Kinetics)

Food for fitness Anita Bean (A&C Black)

The New Glucose Revolution Jennie Brand-Miller *et al* (Publishers Group West)

The Complete Guide to Strength Training Anita Bean (A&C Black)

Sport Stretch Michael J Alter (Human Kinetics)

The Complete Guide to Stretching Christopher Norris (Lyons Press)

Strong to the Core Lisa Westlake (Aurum Press)

Fitness and Health Brian Sharkey (Human Kinetics)

Sports Injuries (A Self Help Guide) Vivian Grisogono (John Murray)

Running Fitness and Injuries Vivian Grisogono (John Murray)

Jump Rope Training Buddy Lee (Human Kinetics)

Athletic Abs Cole and Seabourne (Human Kinetics)

Sports Massage Yinen and Cash (Ebury Press)

First Aid Manual St. John's Ambulance (Dorling Kindersley)

For hard gainers only:

Brawn Stuart McRobert (Common Sense Publishing)

Beyond Brawn Stuart McRobert (Common Sense Publishing)

Models

My heartfelt thanks go out to all of our models and our excellent photographer, Pete Drinkell.

Corey Donoghue

Owen Ogbourne

Wayne Rowlands

Howard Newton

David Thorp

Victoria Mose

Samantha Russell

Steve Wright

Dave Birkett

Tanya Rahman

Oliver Sebe

Lora Venables